Hybrid H
Scient
of Our 00-
Year-Old Alien
Legacy

Daniella Fenton

ISBN: 9781980846604

Dedication

With love to the three beautiful souls that came to earth through me, Camilla, Ariane, Zackary, and all the children of Earth.

Epigraph

"The scientific community explains everything away by nothing else but natural selection and coincidence, and the intelligent design camp suggests everything was done by God. What if this external force did indeed exist, but it may have been an extraterrestrial."

– Giorgio Tsoukalos

Table of Contents

Preface

There are few subjects as fascinating to explore as aliens. We freely ponder the nature of such entities, the craft they might use and what kind of the interactions our had between them and humans. Not least we wonder about the agendas extraterrestrial beings could have in respect to this planet. Notice here that I don't start with the question of whether aliens exist or not, being personally convinced of an affirmative answer by my own experiences.

I am a life-long experiencer of so-called *supernatural* events and work as a psychic medium, regression therapist and licenced practitioner of Andean shamanism. In my professional activities, I have had communication with deceased humans and non-human entities. These contacts are both extraterrestrial and interdimensional in nature. If you speak to any psychic medium or shaman and ask them whether they have received communications from beings identifying themselves as alien to this world, it is almost sure they will confirm they have. Contact with such entities is a frequent occurrence in the psychical community.

Some of my earliest memories, from around 18 months old, include profoundly strange beings in the area just beyond my cot. I recall many, many, times when bizarre creatures were with me in my room. One of these beings was a hairy ape-like humanoid, it stood a little over one metre in height and had the disconcerting habit of bouncing around the room. It was no less frightening to observe it standing at the corner of my cot watching me. I was left me to wonder if it might grab hold of me at any moment. I saw this same ape-like entity dozens and dozens of times over a period of several years. If that does not sound bad enough, there was also another visitor to my bedroom that would leave me trembling in my bed while it stood still monitoring me. This second entity was almost two metres tall, greyish-black, with almond-shaped eyes.

Some will say that these nocturnal visits were merely the vivid dreams of a child, simply fantasies rather than phantasms. My response to such dismissals would be to highlight the fact that for my entire life since then I have continued to see non-human entities and spirit people. I see such apparitions very frequently and not always at night.

Perhaps among the strangest of my experiences are the dozens of spontaneous shamanic journeys that occurred during the year 2012. These fully immersive events involved my falling unconscious on my bed before finding myself inhabiting the body of a lady living in the Mayan city of Palenque in the 7th century, during the rule of Lord Janaab Pakaal. The leadership of the Mayan city, including Pakaal and the lady I had morphed into, were revealed to be alien-human hybrids.

Over the course of my journeys to Palenque, I was given a great deal of information, some of which could be considered extraterrestrial knowledge. One of the most important revelations that emerged was the location from which the aliens had travelled to our world, which lay in the direction of the Pleiades star cluster.

Now, whether this was indeed a past life experience or a case of astral time-travel to the real city of Palenque, I can't be entirely sure. Perhaps my journeys involved some strange alien projection of that city beamed into my consciousness, like a bizarre virtual reality game. I have no way to tell such profoundly strange possibilities one from the other and will merely say that these were a vividly real experience that happened to me. They have changed my life forever, not necessarily in a wholly positive way. I will never again be the person I was before these fantastical trips unfolded.

Apart from shamanic type voyages involving an alien intelligence, I have also witnessed what would probably now be termed UAV's (Unidentified Aerial Vehicles). I would like to share one of these here as it had a profound impact on me and remains my most vivid encounter with something I consider to be advanced technology from beyond this world.

My encounter with a strange aerial craft, or three of them, happened back in 1999. This occurred in the late evening as I drove with my father between Sydney city centre towards the airport tunnel, we saw cars slowing down as though there had been an accident. We slowed down and noticed people were getting out of their cars and looking up at the sky. We stopped and did the same thing. We then saw, immediately above the control tower of the airport, three triangular objects hovering in a triangle formation. Each object had a light on its three points and another in the centre that pulsed slowly and off. After about five minutes the craft shot off away from each other in three separate directions.

My dad got us back in the car, and we drove into the nearby tunnel bypass. Upon exiting again we noticed one of the three objects was now above our car. We followed the grand parade to Brighton le Sands, a small beachside suburb, and then continued driving for about 15 minutes. The craft kept close, always about 50 – 100 metres above us. It eventually made a closer approach, trees lining the road seemed to keep it limited to their topmost heights. After the object moved towards us, we noticed that our car radio began making strange noises. Our car's engine also seemed to be affected by the thing above us as it started producing some peculiar sounds.

I told my dad to pull into a nearby McDonalds before we potentially broke down. It was only at this stage that the craft began to lift away vertically before shooting off at break-neck speed.

I was only after the strange triangle had vanished that my father admitted to me he had seen things a bit like this before when he was just a young man still living in his native Ecuador. On one occasion he was among a crowd that witnessed a strange craft stationary high above the cathedral in his hometown, Ambato. The other instances of unusual aerial phenomena all occurred while he was working in the Ecuadorian jungles, these included glowing orbs following his vehicle at night.

Due to all these experiences and many others too long to list here, I am a convinced of the existence of extra-terrestrial and inter-dimensional intelligence. My personal experiences have also encouraged me to be open-minded towards claims made by other people, whether they claim psychic transmissions, personal encounters, abduction events, or the witnessing of strange visitors to our world traversing the night sky.

Many researchers have collected evidence of historical UFO visitations and ongoing modern ET encounters. Some of the data recorded by investigators suggested that aliens have frequently been visiting this planet for most of the last century. It also appears that these visitors continue to fly through our skies as they please, even taking abductees with impunity whenever desired. Many books address this type of UFO and alien evidence, and it is not my intention to repeat a task already completed by others better suited to it. I am not a ufologist nor am I involved in researching the alien abduction phenomena. I have had my personal experiences in those areas, but that is it.

My own interest in the arena of extraterrestrial and interdimensional intelligence is in attempting to validate claims of direct contact in prehistoric times. The period I will be focusing on lays so long ago that you might think my task impossible. Indeed, under ordinary circumstances and limited to mundane lines of evidence I am sure this task would be impossible. As you will come to see, it is due to my privileged access to some quite extraordinary sources that this project is made feasible. I am sure that this sounds cryptic in the extreme, but all will be made clear as we progress.

Hybrid Humans: Scientific Evidence of our 800,000-Year-Old Alien Legacy is a very different book to any that has preceded it in the extraterrestrial genre. We will explore a compelling witness account involving interactions with a purported alien artefact and analyse the recovered past-life memories of over thirty people. From the information these unusual sources provide, I will attempt to validate the most significant central claims with objective scientific evidence.

As an experienced shaman, psychic medium and certified past life regression therapist, I find myself in an excellent position to explore these types of accounts. However, it is mostly thanks to the close support of my husband and fellow researcher, Bruce Fenton, that I have access to an extensive body of scientific research to cross-reference. Bruce is the author of *The Forgotten Exodus: The Into Africa Theory of Human Evolution* a pop-science book which explores the human origins narrative. The result of fusing these various lines of evidence together is a solid scientific argument for an advanced cosmic civilisation having visited this planet hundreds of thousands of years ago. More importantly, and perhaps even more controversial, we contend that these visitors helped to engineer the early ancestors of *Homo sapiens*.

Daniella Fenton

Bathurst, Australia, 2018

Acknowledgements

I would like to offer my thanks to my husband, Bruce, for his tireless efforts in tracking down the supporting scientific information required for this project. My highest appreciation is reserved for Valerie Barrow for giving permission to use material and quotes (one begins each chapter) from her book, *Alcheringa...when the first ancestors were created*. Valerie's book acted as a roadmap for my investigation. A special thank you to William Brown, the head physicist at the Resonance Science Foundation, for his kindly offered thoughts on advanced space travel technologies. I would also like to extend my gratitude to Leonard Farra for sending us his books to explore, which are mentioned in the early part of this journey. To all those not named here but who kindly gave their time and thoughts during my research, please know that you are all very much appreciated!

Introduction

Not long ago the famous magazine *New Scientist* offered a list of the most significant questions being asked by people today. At number one on that list was perhaps the most significant question any of us can ask, 'What is reality?', but one question was notable by its absence, 'Are we alone in the universe?'

Every living human being with sufficient brain function and sensory input will likely wonder to themselves, at least once, whether intelligent life exists somewhere beyond this plant. It is a question that has played on the minds of leading scientists from many fields and troubled the thoughts of philosophers and theologians. It is this exciting possibility which has driven artists and writers to create marvellous, fantastical, depictions of possible alien beings.

Academics have applied all the existing scientific knowledge to the question of whether we might one day encounter an advanced extraterrestrial civilisation. The mechanisms associated with life on earth have been examined from within the major scientific disciplines of biology, chemistry and physics. The data produced has then been meshed with every finding from the space sciences of astrophysics and exobiology. Complex math formulas have been used to calculate the number of habitable planets and the chances of life emerging and reaching complexity. Philosophers and psychologists have even modelled possible examples of alien cultures and the way they might structure their civilisations.

The results of all this dedicated activity can be summed up as a complex mixture of hope-filled optimism and woeful pessimism. Many of the scientists at the alien hunting organisation SETI are confident that within the next few decades there will be the detection of chemical signatures for organic life. Such discoveries would come thanks to technologies being used to analyse the atmospheric composition of distant worlds. Perhaps we even may yet pick up a stray radio signal from advanced beings on a distant planet.

Some scientists suspect that life on Earth may be unique, an anomaly in an otherwise barren universe. Indeed, a lack of life out there in the cosmos is an excellent explanation for why scientists have so far found nobody out there. No matter how many scientists you speak to it is likely you will discover few who believe humanity will have a direct encounter with advanced extraterrestrial beings any time soon.

The reason for the perceived low chances of humanity contacting other complex life forms, scattered among the stars comes down to several basic understandings and a couple of significant assumptions. The first considerations are that the physical universe is vast and ancient. This immense size and deep antiquity favour any civilizations being separated both by enormous distance and time.

With so many potential target star systems to examine, it is seen as mathematically unlikely that we, or any intelligent race, would be lucky enough to target one of the planets home to complex organisms. The fact that the universe has been around for billions of years allows for a civilization to have emerged and collapsed before any attempt to seek it out even begins.

When all these considerations are factored in, we can understand why there is scientific scepticism surrounding the possibility of contacting alien beings in the imminent future. Scientists are aware it would take a great deal of luck to stumble on any advanced civilizations. The inherent need for us to beat all the odds plays both ways, even with two distinct parties dedicated to searching out the other the mathematical chances favour them missing each other.

We now need to look a little bit closer at one of the core assumptions at the foundation of the human quest to find friends out in the cosmos.

Human scientists assume that the aliens are unaware humanity has emerged. This assumption, if true, requires the extraterrestrial race to somehow stumble on our existence. It is this assumption, a seemingly reasonable one, which is the central cause of all the pessimism among interested academics. The question we need to ask is, what if an extraterrestrial intelligence had known for millions of years that our planet harboured organic life?

In this book, you will be presented with stunning evidence which strongly suggests our Earth has been known to extraterrestrial races right from the moment life appeared here. In fact, it will be argued that an alien civilization likely seeded our world with DNA based organisms. This planting of life on Earth would have taken place shortly after the planet's crust solidified.

The delivery of life to our young world would have established a cosmic relationship with extraterrestrial progenitors from the very first moment of planetary genesis. Though the scientific argument for such a seeding event is not new, termed directed panspermia, the evidence has increased over time.

If advanced beings were aware that our planet housed life long before humans even emerged, suddenly all the complex calculations and accrued science data would tell us absolutely nothing about the likelihood of advanced beings turning up on our doorstep. We would instead need to consider whether a galactic intelligence had been quietly monitoring this world and taking an interest in the evolution of life on its surface.

The evidence I have gathered goes even further than supporting the radical possibility of directed panspermia. I contend that a specific group of extraterrestrial beings involved themselves directly in the evolution of early hominins ancestral to our *Homo sapiens* species. Comprehensible and logical reasons for this interference in our natural development will be identified and explained. You will not be required to take the opinions of others on faith, or to accept arcane ancient texts and megalithic structures as suitable supporting evidence.

For the first time in human history, we will reveal compelling scientific evidence for an extraterrestrial craft visiting this planet in prehistory. Provided for your consideration is the detailed scientific analysis of material remains associated with the advanced alien starship. In all instances where scientific opinions are taken, they are those of highly respected academic researchers.

In respect to the argument that human evolution had a helping hand, you will be offered a detailed analysis of anomalies in the human genome. It is my conclusion that these genetic anomalies confirm deliberate engineering of the hominin species ancestral to early *Homo sapiens*. It will be hard to accept at this stage, but the book in your hands provides tangible objective proof that we are not alone in the vastness of space.

Before digging into the hard science, we will first explore a significant body of material that confirms these extraterrestrial beings are engaged in a very gradual process of initiating an inter-stellar relationship with humanity. This interaction takes the form of a gradually evolving contact continuum. This incremental process is so esoteric and alien in nature that our planetary population has mostly failed to recognise its existence.

Humans tend to mistakenly assume that an alien civilisation would make contact in a way that would be obvious to everybody. Perhaps they will land on the White House lawn and shake hands with the president. We are dealing with an entirely unknown and mysterious type of consciousness. The alien intelligence currently making contact with humanity evolved in a wildly different situation and over a vastly extended period. This extraterrestrial collective possesses technological creations and psychical capabilities which appear magical to humans.

This book provides all the evidence required to accept the stunning revelation that we have at least one group of friends beyond this world. These beings are making it apparent that they stand ready for us to offer our hand in greeting but will do nothing to prompt the impression that they are intent on invading our planet.

This is not strictly a book only about aliens and the strange ways in which they behave or their spectacular abilities/technologies. We will take a very close look at human beings and the backstory to how we came to be as we are. In the final chapter, we will explore the enormous impact of the genetic engineering carried out in prehistory. In understanding what was done and the results it had we can learn a great deal more about ourselves.

Not only have our genes and physical form been profoundly influenced by the intervention event, but even the very foundations of human social behaviour were laid down for us. There is a great deal of 'humanness' that we owe to our extraterrestrial relatives.

Chapter 1 –The First Contact Continuum

"The star people eventually died, but not before telling them that they would return one day."

Humans have long looked up at the heavens and wondered about any beings that might live out there among the stars. Most ancient cultures have passed down stories of gods and spirits that populate the inky blackness of the night sky or reside on far-off worlds. The earliest spiritual traditions, commonly bundled together under the word *shamanism*, included the understanding that humans could contact some of these entities inhabiting the sky worlds. It was widely accepted that psychical voyagers could bring back useful information from these metaphysical interactions.

If the contact claims offered by shamanic cultures are based on fact, which many of us believe they are, then the first contact between modern humans and extraterrestrial entities likely happened many millennia ago. It is possible the first exchange between us and extraterrestrials was initiated by a shaman entering into an altered state of consciousness and subsequently visiting a neighbouring dimension.

Having had many such encounters with non-human entities during my own shamanic practices, I have no reason to doubt the validity of the experiences of other ancestral healers and mystics. It is crucial to point out here that not all aliens need be physical beings, some could reside outside of the constraints of our physical universe, existing as discarnate intelligence.

In our modern world, most people tend to imagine the first contact between our species and advanced alien races involving nuts and bolts type scenarios. Perhaps the most common depiction is that of the interstellar vehicle landing on the White House lawn, with some humanoid being coming out to shake hands with the president of the United States (representing the most powerful human). Though the specifics of this initial meeting vary, a great many people expect first contact akin to how we greet people on our own planet.

We humans usually physically go to where the other person is that we want to meet, generally in some type of transportation device. Upon arrival, we announce ourselves and then have a face-to-face physical interaction with them. The reality is that assuming this is what an alien would do is just a projection of human thinking. We should be wary of our seemingly reasonable expectations being overlaid onto an intelligence that has no experience of human cultural norms. Most scientists and psychologists working on the question of ET contact tend to see this as the most unlikely type of first contact.

Second in popularity only to the direct open visitation, is the expectation that first contact will involve one of our advanced listening stations. It could be perhaps that a radio-telescope picks up a signal from deep space being emitted by another technological species. The message received might be a deliberate greeting sent to us, or it could be an intercepted communication intended for other members of the originating species.

The Search for Extraterrestrial Intelligence project (S.E.T.I.) works to monitor the cosmos for any errant signals which show signs of order or intentional structure. There have already been a few tantalising detection success stories, but unfortunately, unless a message repeats it is not possible to designate it as artificial in nature. To date, we do not have convincing evidence of any repeating synthetic transmission among those received.

Have you ever wondered what an extraterrestrial first contact event might smell Like?

That may seem like an obtuse question, but while there is always a great deal of speculation on how visitors from space would psychically present themselves we really should be thinking outside of the box. It is probable you have never given much thought to what role smell might play in such a situation. It seems out of context thinking perhaps, yet this is entirely why such a question should be asked. Extraterrestrial beings would likely behave in ways outside of our expectations and even beyond our comprehension, indeed, their behaviour would be entirely 'alien'.

If we make the mistake of expecting an extraterrestrial to behave just like a human and to utilise greeting methods identical to our we could easily mistake contact for something else. In fact, our naïve expectations could ensure we miss an attempted greeting entirely. We know that even among animals on this planet many utilise smell or displays of colour to greet fellow members of their species. Certain animals produce sounds which would be inaudible to humans, others emit invisible pheromones as their standard method of welcoming. To be ready for communication from alien beings we must think entirely outside the box. I would implore you to open your mind to an unlimited range of potential contact scenarios. Perhaps the one constant in any hypothetical model for such an event should be the expectation for some degree of high-strangeness.

Fortunately, there are several useful depictions of extraterrestrial contact scenarios available from within the modern popular culture. There are five Hollywood films that I would like to highlight here for your consideration, each of which had considerable input from scientists and prominent thinkers, as well as including a good dose of creative genius.

The plots I would like to highlight each ask audiences to forget about the 'landing on the White House lawn' scenario and instead consider much more likely possibilities. It is also my opinion that each of these stories includes a degree of overlap with the real-life extraterrestrial contact events which will be discussed later in this book. Consider this slight diversion a preparation for the journey ahead. As weird as the stories told in these movies might be I would remind you that truth is often stranger than fiction. It is also my personal suspicion that some of the material contained in the following stories may have been seeded by people 'in the know' as the overlaps are just so close I struggle to accept them as entirely coincidental.

The first movie I want to mention is Steven Spielberg's classic, *Close Encounters of the 3rd Kind* (1977). In this production, we are presented with a multi-levelled contact scenario involving a wide range of strange phenomenon. The initial events of the film include the sudden reappearance of several planes and boats long vanished inside the infamous Bermuda Triangle.

The circumstances surrounding the reappeared craft are investigated by a team of scientists and ufologists. This team of experts are led to an encounter with a group of spiritual adepts in India. The Indian monks are chanting a series of weird sounds which they claim to have heard coming down from the sky. The same sequence of tones is later broadcast into space by a research team in the United States. The interstellar message prompts a reply from an unknown intelligence incorporating a set of coordinates for a location in Wyoming.

Meanwhile, in Muncie, Indiana, there is a visitation involving strange aerial craft emitting flashing coloured lights. These unidentified flying objects cause much chaos, including disrupting the power grid. While working on the resultant problems, a local electrician, Roy Neary, has a close encounter with one of the craft. This interaction between Roy and the object provokes and obsessed state, it seems some thoughtform has been embedded in his mind. Roy goes on to construct a model of a mountain that he keeps on seeing inside his head, the model strangely matches an image of

Devil's Mountain, Wyoming, shown on his television.

Roy is compelled to reach the off-limits landing site on Devil's mountain, while on-route he discovers that many other alien contactees have also received the message and are trying to access the location. The film climaxes with the alien mothership arriving and a series of exchanged sound and light communications between the ground and the craft. The vessel lands and the door open allowing several previously abducted humans to emerge. Roy is then cleared to join a group of scientists that have decided to depart with the extraterrestrial visitors to learn more from them.

Though perhaps somewhat dated as a film, *Close Encounters of the 3rd Kind* gives a good sense of the type of phenomenon we might expect to accompany a greeting from beyond the stars. We are given a show of power by the beings, an unequivocal demonstration of their superior technologies alongside a method for responding to them. Importantly the creatures show no interest in meeting a singular leader. While the extraterrestrials do communicate with the local power structures (mainly government scientists), they also send psychic invitations to a broad segment of the public. In a final overt show of their benevolent intentions, the aliens return everyone they have ever abducted for study. Finally, there is an offering of a personnel exchange to formalise the future working relationship between species. All the phenomena in the film, though replete with high strangeness, start to make sense once put together into the context of advanced aliens making their first contact.

Another movie that comes to my mind is *Contact* (1997), based on a book of the same name written by the famous astrophysicist, Carl Sagan. The story centres around Dr Ellie Arroway, a scientist involved with SETI who finds a repeating signal. The source of the emission is in the direction of the star Vega, situated in the constellation of Lyra.

The intercepted message contains a hidden schematic for a huge machine. The device is eventually constructed by the allied governments of the world working in harmony. The mechanism appears to be designed to allow one occupant to enter inside and presumably contact those sending the messages. In an unexpected turn of events, a religious fanatic carries out a suicide bomb attack on the installation destroying it and killing the chosen passenger.

Fortunately, the destruction of the mysterious machine is not the end of the story as a reclusive billionaire has privately funded a backup copy of the machine. It is this secret project which eventually allows Ellie to operate the device, which, as it transpires, can move her through space and time.

After passing through a series of wormholes, a meeting takes place between Ellie and a non-physical extraterrestrial being presenting itself in the form of her deceased father. The climax of the film takes place on a beach that is being projected to Ellie based on memories extracted from her own mind. The alien being provides little more than confirmation that there are many advanced races in the universe, explaining that they contact progressive species whenever it seems appropriate. It is made apparent that humanity is not considered enlightened enough to gain immediate admission into their galaxy-wide network. The being clarifies that Earth will be monitored until such time that another step can be taken towards friendship.

We can recognise in *Contact* several essential themes, firstly a comprehensible caution on behalf of the extraterrestrial entities who want to take gradual steps. The aliens initiate monitoring of our planet while they take time to consider full contact between their species and ours. The mode of transport they utilise is wormhole-based. Wormholes are a theoretical method of moving vast distances quickly and can potentially even move an object through time. We are also introduced to the idea of secret projects involving advanced alien technologies run by shady billionaires. This suggestion of secret scientific projects is something many people suspect is happening on Earth today.

Two much more recent films that are also important to consider, *Interstellar* (2014) and *Arrival* (2016). These films both involve the manipulation of time by highly advanced technologies. There is a puzzle set by the beings requiring humanity to find the very best in themselves. Not only do we see some novel ideas presented, but also advances in modern scientific understanding are reflected in the plots.

In *Interstellar* the beings involved are eventually deduced to be descendants of modern humans now existing in a fifth dimension. These distant relatives have reached back through time to help their ancestors (creating several temporal paradoxes in the process).

The extraterrestrial beings in the movie *Arrival* are also deeply involved in the manipulation of time. These octopus-like entities have seen a future timeline upon which humans will do something to save their species. Initially, the creatures position several of their craft around the planet and then wait to see if humanity can solve a puzzle they have set. The only way for we humans to progress the contact is by all the countries uniting in a collective effort. This process of distributing necessary clues ensures a global communication rather than a dialogue with any singular power or individual.

Both *Arrival* and *Interstellar* suggest that genuinely advanced civilisations will have some degree of control over time itself. These films also suggest that contact with an incredibly sophisticated technological culture is likely to revolve around their self-interests. We should carefully consider the motivations of any species that reaches out across the cosmos to shake our hands. It is likely the motivations for comic contact would be benevolent, but they could involve more negative intentions. Admittedly, it might be hard for us to do much about any evil plans formulated by a highly advanced galactic civilization.

Many of the concepts and specific details presented in these four Hollywood movies also feature in the real-life contact event discussed in this book. The beings encountered undoubtedly have a level of self-interest. These entities control technologies which allow them to move through time and space. It is my opinion that some of the strange objects in our skies are technologies operated by this cosmic intelligence. Unidentified flying objects may be a visual demonstration of the power wielded by off-world or interdimensional forces.

It is also possible that these non-human beings are in contact with government agencies, unknown to us. I suspect they might be, but clearly, they are also making contact with members of the general public through psychical mechanisms. It is my strongest suspicion that once we as a global species recognise and acknowledge their invitation to communicate, a straightforward and overt relationship will be established.

I can't close this chapter without mentioning one last film, *2001: A Space Odyssey* (1968). The first thing that should be said about this film is that the scriptwriters, Stanley Kubrick and Arthur C. Clarke are known to have had some incredibly well-positioned friends. It is no great stretch to imagine that they could have heard about any secret projects involving extraterrestrial beings. What is certain is the film is rife with esoteric occult symbolism. The script contains a narrative with considerable overlaps between it and the non-fiction events I focus on in my investigation. These two men seemingly knew something of the matter at hand, of that I have little doubt.

The film *2001: A Space Odyssey* reveals that an advanced extraterrestrial intelligence sent a technological device to Earth in prehistory. The alien machine is in the form of a giant black obsidian-like monolith. In the initial scenes of the movie, ancient hominins encounter the monolith during a cosmic convergence. Proximity to the monolith somehow modifies human consciousness, as we discover in the next segment of the film.

The group of hominids affected by the alien technology spontaneously start using animal bones as clubs. The wielding of the first weapons signifies the initiation of a path towards human technological superiority. One of the bone clubs is thrown into the air and as we watch it rise the scene cuts, and the club is replaced in the frame by an advanced orbital weapons platform.

Later on in the screenplay, a second monolith is encountered hidden on the moon. Astronauts touching this new monolith cause a signal to be emitted from it towards Jupiter. We are left to assume the monolith is informing its mysterious creators that humanity has moved out beyond the stars.

Having tentatively explored some hypothetical alien contact scenarios I would like to lay my cards on the table, so to speak. It is my informed opinion that there is substantial evidence of the first contact between humans and extraterrestrial beings occurring hundreds of thousands of years ago. Not only has communication with humanity already begun but it is ongoing. Much of the interaction between the aliens and humans occurs in non-physical reality with the human participants being in altered states of consciousness. Some such contacts even happen while people are in dream states.

Extraterrestrial contact is not an isolated event, it is a continuum, and we are a long way into this process already. In fact, we are about to reach a crucial advanced stage on this path. The next step forward involves widespread human acceptance of the existence of alien civilisations, based on objective evidence. If this happens and is followed by a public call for fully visible meetings with this cosmic intelligence, it will give the green light to benevolent extraterrestrial cultures to fully reveal themselves. We may well be at the beginning of the real space age in which humanity begins open, overt, relationships with our extraterrestrial and interdimensional intelligence.

Chapter 2 –The Alien Artefact

"One of the first things that he communicated was knowledge that the Alcheringa stone was brought to Earth by an extraterrestrial culture known as the 'Star People'."

From the early part of 2012 until 2013, while I was living in Ecuador, I went through a series of mind-bending and incredibly stressful extraterrestrial contact experiences. These events did not involve aliens landing their saucers in my garden or them sucking me out of the bedroom window. That does not mean these events were any less tangible, and they were undoubtedly equally bizarre. The things I went through have changed me as a person forever, both my perception of reality and my personal health have been considerably impacted. I need to share just the barest of details of these strange events here, solely matters which tie into our investigation. There is far more to my personal story than I can share here as it would end up doubling the length of this book.

On the very first of these strange journeys, I found myself in a circular and domed space, in hindsight I wonder if it could have been a craft. I can't say for sure where I was during the experience. Present with me were several humanoid and very human-like beings. These beings were very tall and quite obviously not of this world. Most of the people were engaged in a discussion about Earth and various events currently unfolding or expected to occur in the future. Quite honestly, at this point, I assumed I was probably dead. You see, before appearing in this strange meeting I had collapsed on my bed in absolute agony, finally passing out before feeling myself broken into tiny pieces which were the dragged through my bedroom wall. The shocking transition from my physical life to this bizarre, and equally real, other-dimensional realm was just so incredibly painful. It was a level and type of pain I will never forget.

While my personality, that intangible part of myself had been pulled out of mundane reality, my physical body remained in bed, visible to Bruce. This was the case for all the dozens of similar voyages that would follow over the months ahead. The second time these beings dragged my point of awareness away from my mundane existence I found myself inhabiting a new body. The person I had 'become' was an extremely tall and powerful young woman wearing very tribal Indian type clothes.

It did not take me too long to uncover that the women I was inhabiting was a noble of the Maya elite in the city of Palenque, Mexico. At a later stage in these experiences, I came to understand that the events were unfolding during the 7th century AD. This noblewoman was not a typical human being, she apparently had an extra dash of alien DNA. Indeed, most of the highest dignitaries in Palenque seemed to be of the same hybrid race as my personal 'avatar'. These 'people' were generally around two metres tall, essentially giants compared to the regular Maya citizens. Much of the official business of the city was conducted during meetings in a subterranean tunnel network. The Mayan underground was filled with calendars, artefacts, tablets - incredible wonders.

I spent just over a year living two distinct lives, each separated by several centuries but linked by a thread of shared high strangeness. As a life-long psychic medium, I have experienced decades of supernormal phenomena. My strange experiences include everything from seeing spirits to channelling ascended masters. These shamanic journeys, or whatever they should be called, are the most bizarre of all the phenomena that have featured in my life so far.

Living among the Maya-alien hybrids was not the only thing to contend with in Palenque. In a separate section of the underground network, there were experimental laboratories run by some very different beings. The residents of these chambers were very intimidating, tall, grey-skinned, humanoids. I come to refer to these characters as tall greys. Working alongside these oversized creatures were what appeared to be much smaller versions of themselves.

On several occasions I noticed one other type of humanoids in this part of the tunnel system, these were very human-like, but with scaly skin that reminded me of lizards. My assumption is these were hybrids of humans and some other extraterrestrial race. The Maya leadership were associated with entities linked to the Pleiades star cluster, it was not made clear what cosmic locations these other beings were associated with.

Many of my unusual experiences were shared in a book I co-authored with Bruce titles *2012 Rising - The Last Tzolkin: Warnings From The Maya & The Pleiadians* (2012). One of the readers of that book recognised a connection between some of our published accounts and the work of an Australian research team, Steven and Evan Strong. Communication was established with these team, and after some conversations, we all decided to work on a book together. This collaborative relationship resulted in us co-authoring the book *Ancient Aliens In Australia: Pleiadian Origins of Humanity* (2013).

Without this profoundly strange chain of events, we would never have ended up doing the research contained in the current book. I now understand that my shamanic journeys to Palenque were yet another facet of this extraterrestrial contact continuum. No matter how odd the individual events involved, there is a more coherent bigger picture visible once we zoom out and see things in their entirety.

During the latter part of the writing process, one of my fellow co-authors mentioned a book called *ALCHERINGA...When the first ancestors were created* (2002). They revealed that it was the overlap between my personal experiences and the content of that book, which had convinced them we should work together on the a book. Bruce bought a copy of the Alcheringa book from its author, Valerie Barrow, and read the entire book out loud so we would both know what it was all about.

In all fairness, you can probably get some idea of what *ALCHERINGA...When the first ancestors were created* is about just from reading that title. The core of the story claimed extraterrestrial involvement in the origins of modern humans. The author, Valerie Barrow, is an Australian psychic medium. Bruce and I were both amazed that this book involved the same types of entities that had been involved in my own otherworldly experiences. It seemed Valerie had uncovered a great deal of information related to an ET hybridisation program on this planet. Despite an almost complete lack of objective evidence to support the events described in the book we suspected it detailed many actual occurrences from the remote past.

Bruce admits to having had a particularly strong emotional reaction to Valerie Barrow's manuscript, especially when it detailed the destruction of an alien mothership. This enormous craft had been in orbit above Earth, with thousands of peaceful travellers on board.

Bruce explained to me that it reminded him of a powerful past-life memory he had experienced during a personal shamanic journey back in 2002 (coincidently the same year the Alcheringa book was published). During the fully immersive experience, Bruce found himself as a tall extraterrestrial humanoid in a blue uniform, piloting a small space-craft towards Earth. Just behind the ship, several hostile craft were in pursuit.

While still in this visionary state Bruce experienced an intense and painful knowing that a terrible disaster had claimed the lives of 'his' comrades. These beings had come in peace to assist the Earth. Almost all of them had died in flames, their ship destroyed in the inky blackness of space.

Bruce's experience during his shamanic journey mesh incredibly with the story told in Valerie's book. It turns out he is not the only person to recall piloting a spacecraft towards Earth after a surprise catastrophe. This synchronistic past-life memory was yet another prompt for me to take the accounts shared in the Alcheringa book into serious consideration.

We have since met Valerie Barrow, and her husband John, they were kind enough to have our family visit them for lunch at their home in late 2016. I knew from that meeting that Valerie is a lovely lady and a kindred spirit. I felt very comfortable sharing a conversation with her about our respective lifetimes of supernormal experiences. We certainly had a great many things in common!

After our visit to Valerie, Bruce and I began to wonder whether it might be possible to track down any tangible evidence which could validate *ALCHERINGA...When the first ancestors were created*. It occurred to us that while there might not have been any supporting material evidence when the book was published in 2002, perhaps in the subsequent years the situation could have changed. Might advances in biological sciences and archaeology provide at least some direct evidence?

Before providing our validation of the accounts offered by Valerie Barrow, we must first introduce a little of her material. While it is not essential to have read *ALCHERINGA…When the first ancestors were created* before reading the remainder of this book, it certainly helps to have a copy available. I am only going to be sharing a basic overview and highlighting the most spectacular claims. My focus is on those elements which I identified as being essential to validate.

The opening events in Valerie's book occurred in the mid-1990s and involved the arrival of an ancient artefact to her home. At this time Valerie was living in a house she had named *Alcheringa*, this is an Australian Aboriginal word from the Central and Northern Territories regions. The word Alcheringa refers to the period in which the first ancestors of humanity were created by powerful cosmic spirits, also more widely known as the *Dreamtime*. The word Alcheringa is closely related to the term *churinga*[1] which denotes a sacred artefact that is imbued with secret messages.

Churingas can take different forms, but usually, they are portable artefacts of wood or stone. Typically, these objects are decorated with sacred symbols and markings. It is understood by Aboriginal people that a churinga carries privileged information reserved only for elders and spiritual initiates. Among the Aboriginal nations who possess Churinga, it is also believed that some of the stone examples are incredibly ancient. The eldest of all these stone artefacts are considered to be imbued with the life-force of ancestral spirits from the 'Alcheringa' period, the time before time. These Alcheringa spirits can purportedly take human incarnations while still having some part of their soul remaining rooted in the matrix of their stone receptacle.

Though today many churinga stones are acknowledged to be replicas of the original ones, since lost (still highly sacred even then), it seems that the one which reached Valerie was no recent replication. Through a chain of synchronicity involving her house name, a lady named Helen Boyd heard about Valerie. One day Helen came to visit Valerie and suggested that because of her house's name she was the right person to temporarily look after a sacred object. It was hoped that Valerie would act as a temporary custodian while arrangements were made for this artefact to reach the correct Aboriginal caretakers.

Helen was very unwell, and Valerie took pity on her situation, agreeing to keep the artefact in her home until it was again retrieved. At that time, she had no idea it was anything more than an old round stone tightly wrapped in paperbark. Valerie respectfully placed it into a small box and put it away for safekeeping.

It is important to mention here that Valerie never directly looked at this artefact, it always remained within the bark wrapping. This was the culturally sensitive thing to do as these sacred stones are reserved for Aboriginal ceremonial purposes. Even among Aboriginal people only initiated 'clever-fellas', a category of Aboriginal wisdom keeper and shamanic healer, were allowed to handle churinga stones.

Soon after the stone arrived, Valerie was awoken from her sleep by a disembodied voice which asked her if she was ready to write a book. The conversation between Valerie and the discarnate voice continued over time, and she was informed that she was in communication with a 'star person' (extra-terrestrial) connected with the artefact. The entity referred to itself as Alcheringa and claimed that the object in the box was imbued with valuable information, brought to Earth almost 900,000 years ago.

The Alcheringa being initially made itself known via a form of telepathic communication, what might be called psychic mediumship or spiritual channelling. As a psychic medium myself I am intimately familiar with this type of communication process, it can involve what seems to be speech heard only by the channel. It is also possible to receive sensations, vivid imagery or sudden spontaneous 'knowing'. Once this powerful process of communication had been initiated Valerie began to gain an enormous amount of information concerning an ancient extraterrestrial visitation to our planet.

Alcheringa explained to Valerie that she would soon start meeting people connected with the extraterrestrial mission. These other individuals would help to reveal the role this event had played in human origins. This prediction came to pass just as the entity said it would, with over thirty people eventually providing relevant past life memories to the book *Alcheringa...when the first ancestors were created*. Soon after the communication began with Valerie events began to unfold, with plenty of high strangeness.

One of Valerie's friends, Rachel, was passing near to her house while driving with a respected Aboriginal healer, Gerry. Karen mentioned in the car that she had a friend who lived nearby in a house called Alcheringa. At the mention of this Aboriginal word, Gerry suggested that they should make a visit. Valerie was somewhat surprised to meet Gerry, as she had not had much direct contact with Australia's indigenous peoples. That this visit coincided with receiving an Aboriginal sacred artefact seemed to her beyond coincidence.

While talking, Valerie had the sudden strong sense that Gerry already knew that she had the stone and so mentioned it, he immediately snapped back that it was 'men's business'. It is actually true that Churinga stones are only directly handled by initiated men in Aboriginal culture. Once Valerie explained how the rock had come to her, and that it was kept wrapped up and safely secured away in a box, Gerry seemed satisfied. Valerie's offer for Gerry to see the stone was quickly declined, he looked slightly scared by the thought of handling the object, even with it wrapped.

After some conversations about the Alcheringa stone, Gerry mentioned that one of his friends also had interactions with an unseen being that referred to itself as Alcheringa. He then suggested they all visit a sacred site with engraved hieroglyphs located near the town of Gosford, New South Wales. Gerry asked Valerie to bring the artefact as perhaps the voice of the stone would speak to them on-site. Valerie agreed and immediately remembered that Alcheringa had told her that he would one day talk through her to an Aboriginal person.

Today the hieroglyphs engraved on a stone feature near to Gosford have become somewhat famous, but things were not like that when Valerie visited the site over 20 years ago. The rock bluff with these symbols is itself an

Aboriginal site, irrespective of the exact provenance of the hieroglyphs. Many people today consider the glyphs, most of which look Egyptian, to be a peculiar hoax, merely modern additions to an Aboriginal site. There are witness accounts which suggest that some of the symbols are recent creations. However, this hoax claim seems to account for only a proportion of the symbols.

I have visited the Gosford Glyphs myself along with a small group of friends and family, it is in the middle of nowhere. It is indeed an odd place for anyone to plan a hoax as ordinarily such things are done where they will be quickly heard about. Usually, the purpose of such a deception would be to cause a big stir locally, providing the perpetrator with amusement. The location involved in this case is almost impossible to find by accident and hard even when you are looking for it. The engravings are well hidden within a large rocky outcrop and not at all visible even from the small path that winds its way through the surrounding forest.

The only prominent marker for the site is a giant eucalyptus tree, known locally as the grandmother tree. It requires some climbing to reach the small crevasse in which the symbols themselves are on display. I am not a great fan of clambering around on slippery rocks, so I limited myself to peering down at them from a vantage point above, leaving Bruce and our 4-year-old son to do the monkey business of clambering in and taking photos.

While alone I took some time to tune in to the energy of the place and soon had the strong impression that I was in the women's business part of the site and that men should be on the other side. Shortly after this, I noticed a humanoid figure that approached me, it felt like it was the caretaker of the place. This entity checked me out and then moved off heading towards the rest of my group. I was a little worried that it might not be happy with people being there, but nothing happened to anyone.

I looked towards the grandmother tree and instantly felt the presence of three female elders sitting around me, they started talking about the 'time before there was time'. They explained the purpose of the site, which is divided between healing, storytelling and interdimensional travel.

The spirit women started to sing or hum a tune, then a light rain began to fall. It felt very peaceful, and my sense was of having returned to the site after being there long ago. When I started to make my way back down the slippery rocks, carefully, another female spirit emerged and guided me down so that I would not fall. She also had a familiar feel, as though I had some level of kinship with her. There were moments where it felt as though she was holding me steady, it was all very vivid.

When Valerie visited the site for the first time, accompanied by Gerry and her friend Karen, their experiences were somewhat more intense and otherworldly even than my own. After touching the glyphs and then moving to a higher part of the rocky outcrop, Alcheringa spoke through Valerie and announced that he had known the three individuals for many lifetimes. The being continued, explaining that all those present had a direct connection to the Star People.

Alcheringa told them that many of the glyphs had been cut by extraterrestrial beings and that lifeforms from numerous worlds had visited Earth over many millions of years. These visitations involved directly influencing the development of life on this planet. Before departing, Alcheringa mentioned that the glyphs would eventually help to awaken many people.

Gerry then led the trio to a point known as Whale Rock overlooking the Brisbane waters, as they arrived they all began to feel quite peculiar. There was a rock feature which looked like a stone bed melted into a large boulder. This strange stone bed comfortably allowed one person to lay down. Gerry mentioned that in past times Aboriginal women would use this as a birthing place, laying themselves down as they entered labour. Karen promptly lay down within the stone depression and closed her eyes.

The trio shortly found themselves spontaneously shifting into an altered state of consciousness. They were no longer in their natural bodies and the scene around them suggested it was not the present day. Their bodies were now strange alien forms with long slender limbs, light bluish-grey skin and elongated heads. Down in the bay below a crashed saucer-shaped craft was slowly sinking into the water. Above the wrecked ship, another vehicle hovered in the air plucking survivors from the sea. Valerie noticed a pod of dolphins was helping to push some of the floundering beings towards the shore.

This type of vivid experience is known as a spontaneous past life recall, or you might also have heard of these being called time-slips. One moment we are here in the present the next we are a person living in another time. When Bruce and I corresponded with the head of the perceptual studies department at the University of Virginia, Dr Bruce Greyson, he suggested the term retrocognition to describe my personal journeys into the past.

Such events have happened to many people, though not commonly involving extraterrestrial beings, and you can find many relevant books and articles on the subject. It is entirely immersive, you feel that this is a direct real-life experience that you are living, unlike a conventional memory. Having had many such experiences, mostly involving the 7th-century Mayan city of Palenque, I can fully empathise with how Valerie and her friends would have felt. While in the other person's body you also have access to their emotions, thoughts and memories – not just the immediate sensory input. In past life therapy, a healing modality in which I am qualified, people can be deliberately taken through these types of experiences to resolve past-life issues affecting their present-day lives.

Valerie and her two companions experienced being marooned survivors from a mission to Earth. They were aware of a plan which had involved a collective of many benevolent non-human species. The stellar journey had begun in the Pleiades star cluster – even though the various species involved did not necessarily originate in that region of space. Two locations linked to the aliens came to Valerie's mind, one being Lyra and another which sounded somewhat like Altair. Residents of many planetary systems were understood to be involved. The ship had travelled from the Pleiades nebula, being the location of the spatial anomaly which provided the gateway to Earth.

After the shared experience had finished, Valerie pieced together everything she could from her companions including information from a related dream which Gerry had had years before. In Gerry's earlier dream states he had experienced being onboard the mothership as a surprise attack began, with warnings going off around him and, in the panic, he managed to get his family off the endangered vessel. He had piloted a small saucer towards the Earth's surface with others on board, but it crashed into the water near a small beach. In the spontaneous past life experience, Gerry had found himself inside the saucer again, pinned down by part of the damaged craft, slowly drowning. His two otherworldly experiences, one during sleep and another while awake, fitted together perfectly.

Later, Valerie communicated again with Alcheringa to help unravel more of the puzzling events. The story which emerged was that of a sizeable crystalline craft, imbued with its own consciousness, carrying 50,000 colonists from the Pleiades. The plan was to take control of the Earth from its rather unpleasant rulers, successful negotiation had already been completed. Earth would then function as an outpost for benevolent races, keen on assisting with modifying the belief systems of negative intentioned entities inhabiting the surrounding sector of space. Just before taking full control of

Earth, the opposing force of more aggressive extraterrestrials had broken the agreement and launched a surprise attack. Only a handful of scout craft had made it safely down, carrying less than a hundred survivors to the planet's surface.

With their plans in tatters and now lacking the equipment to successfully colonise an environmentally hostile planet, the survivors came up with a new idea. If not for this disaster, and the sudden to revise their plans, modern humans might not exist.

Chapter 3 –Past Life Memories & Alien Messages

"Now I have the mission to tell people of the distant past, and convey the information given to me by others. This is to help bring an understanding of who and what we really are."

Valerie would go on to communicate with Alcheringa many more times before the stone was finally passed back to the Aboriginals. Each occasion added more to the story of the mission from the Pleiades and the marooned survivors on Earth. She also eventually encountered well over twenty people that shared memories of the same series of events. Some had previously experienced dreams about the mission, but most only recalled their past-life memories once shown photographs of the glyphs at Gosford.

More of the story emerged, and it revealed that the surviving star people decided that the only way they could still change Earth's future for the better was by passing on their mission objectives to the most appropriate creature already living on the planet. An upright hairy ape-man was selected for this project, and genetic engineering was commenced. The new modified and hybridised being would in time be suitable for star people to incarnate into, and it would also serve as a vehicle for the souls of other less pleasant cosmic entities. This latter consideration was necessary, the new hybrid had potential beyond that of the local galactic intelligence, which was stuck in a shallow level of consciousness. Incarnation into the new hybrid form would provide a path of upliftment for various negative entities, a chance for these species to evolve spiritually.

You might wonder why the allied forces did not send any rescue attempt, in fact, a fleet of ships arrived five years after the attack. By the time this flotilla of craft reached earth many more of the marooned star people had died, primarily due to their being incredibly poorly suited to the Earth environment. Everything from the intense solar radiation, waterborne bacteria, airborne viruses and poisonous plants had claimed victims. Without all the advanced technologies carried on the mothership, colonisation was utterly impossible. However, the few remaining alive were now committed to helping upgrade the local hominin species. Almost all these survivors declined the offer of rescue and continued working on creating the new human form.

The crews of these newly arrived ships were not colonists, these were warriors from a feline humanoid species (the leonine people). The battlegroup commander issued a final decree to all remaining enemy forces hidden in their underground caverns, to vacate the planet immediately or face the full force of alliance retribution. Though most of the hostile troops withdrew, heading through a gateway to Orion, some refused. The subsequent aerial bombardment of their strongholds was swift and decisive.

Clearly, some of the intricate details which emerge from Valerie's conversations with those involved are beyond anything I can hope to validate. That does not mean they are not right or can't perhaps be proven accurate at some later stage. Equally, I can't say that everything mentioned in her book happened exactly as told. What felt vital to me was that the significant claim that aliens came to earth and helped to direct human evolution was itself something well worth investigating. Eventually, I narrowed down to a few hugely substantial details in the narrative and selected a handful of these critical events which could confirm the visitation. Before going any further let's just quickly go through my target list.

- Provide evidence supporting the claim that Earth was seeded with DNA by an advanced galactic civilisation several billion years ago.

- Provide evidence supporting the claim that extraterrestrial beings could possess technologies capable of travelling across the universe and even through time.

- Provide material evidence proving that a vast crystalline spacecraft exploded in orbit above Australia.

- Provide geological evidence that Earth was deliberately bombarded by asteroids as part of a Pleiadean reprisal for the ambush of their colonists.

- Provide climatic data supporting the claimed severity of the impact of these Pleiadian reprisals stated to have occurred five years after the betrayal.

- Provide detailed genetic information from academic sources that represents evidence of deliberate engineering of ancestral *Homo sapiens*.

- Provide a scientifically well-supported analysis of the impact and implications of the specific modification made to create ancestral *Homo sapiens*.

I freely admit that this sounds like an impossibly ambitious list, but even then, I realised that there was an additional factor to consider, one of timing. This investigation requires one further fixed constraint. All the scientific evidence uncovered needs to point to the same singular period. We have been given a possible date, 900,000 years ago, but I know from my involvement with psychical research that this might be more of a general guide than a fixed signpost. Psychically obtaining precise dates through accessing higher dimensions, many of which exist outside of our linear space-time continuum, is notoriously tricky. That said, this period had come up several times in the book, my thought was that it shouldn't be out by hundreds of thousands of years. For the purposes of our research project, we took this as a guide and began looking at data spanning between 1,000,000 to 800,000 years ago. As it would later turn out, had we not used this more expansive range in our protocol we would have failed to find any proofs.

I am sure that some people will still be struggling with our choice of sources and the idea that a rock could carry the interactive consciousness of an extraterrestrial being or that people can re-experience events from the distant past. While it is correct to say that the validity of these sources can be established by any success we have with using them, it is still well worth us looking closer at expert investigations into these types of phenomena.

Many highly qualified scientists and philosophers have pondered on what to expect from highly advanced extraterrestrial civilisations. We encountered some excellent examples of what alien technologies might be capable of in our earlier look at Hollywood movies. Susan Schneider, a prominent neuroscientist at the University of Pennsylvania, has published some of her thoughts on this matter and she suggests that we should expect some of these beings to have transitioned to a noncorporeal existence or even uploaded their minds into silicon-based networks.[2] A growing number of thinkers in the field of exobiology have concluded that a great many advanced extraterrestrial species would eventually move beyond organic carbon-based forms. We must also consider that the robotic creations of an advanced alien technological culture might be fully sentient and self-aware.

There is as mathematically more chance of us encountering some type of robot than there is of meeting biological aliens. Even biological entities will likely send a robotic probe ahead of any physical visitation to our planet. We use robots to explore and map new environments on Earth as well as space. It may be challenging for us to even recognise an extraterrestrial visitor or even one of their information processing technologies. It might just look some old rock to us.

Some readers may doubt the validity of past life memories as a source for information, however substantial scientific evidence for this has been available for several decades. Professor Ian Stevenson of the University of Virginia's Division of Perceptual Studies conducted detailed academic research into children's memories of recent past lives.

Over the course of some 40 years, Stevenson was able to track down places, people and events that perfectly matched the stories given to him, usually by very young children, in hundreds of cases. Under rigid scientific protocols, a respected and sceptical academic (along with the various international scientists who assisted him), concluded that past life memories genuinely produced historically accurate information in many cases. No matter the exact functioning of the phenomena itself or whatever mechanisms caused it to occur.

For anyone wanting to look more into the evidence of past-life memories providing verifiable data, I recommend looking at Professor Stevenson's vast body of work, which includes around three hundred papers and fourteen books. Stevenson's collection of publications including *Twenty Cases Suggestive of Reincarnation* (1966) and *European Cases of the Reincarnation Type* (2003). Perhaps his most exceptional work is the 2,268-page, two-volume *Reincarnation and Biology: A Contribution to the Etiology of Birthmarks and Birth Defects* (1997). Consider that this masterwork incorporated two hundred cases of birthmarks and birth defects that corresponded to wounds on the deceased person whose life the child recalled. Having read several of his investigative reports, I can only refer to them as stunning and utterly convincing.

Stevenson is not the only scientist or medical professional to stumble into the field of past-life memories and uncover the potential for them to provide detailed accounts of long-distant events. Back in 1962, a highly respected English psychiatrist named Dr Arthur Guirdham was visited by a female patient who was haunted by vivid and violent nightmares. The terrible dreams seemed to centre on some period in ancient history which she could not consciously place.[3]

As Dr Guirdham's patient, Mrs Smith, shared names, details and historical information from her recurrent nocturnal journeys, Guirdham recognised clear links to the Cathars and to the Catholic crusades which eradicated them. The Cathars were considered Christian heretics, at least in the eyes of the Catholic church. Eventually, the inquisition arranged for a bloody invasion of their lands ending in a final barbaric massacre of the surviving men, women and children at Montségur in 1244. The high strangeness had only just begun, the respected psychiatrist, a graduate from the prestigious Oxford University, was about to find himself at the centre of one of the centuries most stunning reincarnation cases.

Soon after Mrs Smith opened up about her troubling visions, several more of his female patients began detailing similar flashbacks. Eventually, Dr Guirdham came to suspect that he was at the centre of something almost unheard of, a case of mass reincarnation. All these patients lived within about 15 miles of the city of Bristol.

Guirdham found that he was also able to recall memories that suggested he had a link to Mrs Smith and the events she described. He set out to unravel the truth of the matter and sifted through all available historical sources. In time, Guirdham successfully identified around a dozen of the names offered to him by his patients. Keep in mind that most of these names linked to unremarkable persons of the 13th century and would not have been known of to these patients. In fact, it took a skilled search through ancient records, helped by reputable historians, to locate these former incarnations listed amongst the records of the French Inquisition. This hardly a source regularly visited by members of the public and I am sure most of us would have no idea such records even existed.

It is worth taking a moment here to highlight some interesting overlaps between Guirdam's story and our own, among these being the fact Bruce and I both consider ourselves to be Gnostic thinkers, as were the Cathars. My grandfather once told me that our family's ancestry traced back to the Cathars in Southern France. Bruce grew up about 30 minutes' drive northeast from where Guirdham's clinic had been, not far from the area where the patients had lived. The most notable connection is in the fact Valerie Barrow has also written about a remembered life as a Cathar initiate, one of those that burned at Montségur. This additional past life account features in her book *TWO SOULMATES ... Walking Through Time & History* (2013). It seems beyond mere coincidence that there would be direct connections between two instances of mass reincarnation, one occurring in England where both Valerie's husband John and my husband Bruce are from, and the other being in Australia where Valerie and I are both native.

Reincarnation is part of various philosophical and spiritual collectives, most famously the Hindus and Buddhists, but it is also a feature of many shamanic traditions and accepted by Gnostics, Celts, Druse and many others.

Collective group reincarnations seem to suggest that there is some other level of order in specific instances of rebirth, perhaps a consciously direct element where some people can choose where, when, and with whom they will be reborn. Tibetan Buddhist masters have long claimed that due to their advanced meditation practices, it is easy for them to choose the details of their subsequent life, and even select the moment of departure. Research into this process, which involves numerous tests to identify returned Buddhist masters, seems to suggest this really can happen.

Even though I am supportive of reincarnation being the best explanation for why many people remember details from lives in the far past, we must keep in mind that we are exploring a rather exceptional instance of retrocognition. This is an instance of humans remembering lives as advanced alien entities. It would be wrong of me to ignore the possibility that other explanations exist for these astonishing memories. We will quickly consider an additional three potential scenarios which might explain, or play some role, in the retrieval of these strange alien memories.

A growing number of neuroscientists and geophysicists are intrigued by the relationship between the workings of the human brain and the electromagnetic field of the planet. In a recent article for the *Scientific and Medical*

Network, the geophysicist, Paul Kieniewicz, discusses the ongoing research into the way our brain might be interacting with natural Earth energies, the title of this piece is *How Private are our Thoughts?*[4]

Kieniewicz explains that in the space between the Earth's surface and the Ionosphere there is a cavity enclosing the Earth's electromagnetic field, in this space there exist extremely low frequencies which form standing waves. These electrical and magnetic standing waves are continually energised by lightning strikes and have resonant peaks at 8Hz, 14Hz, 21Hz and 27Hz. These resonant peaks are best known as Schumann Resonances.

Neurologists have noticed that the electrical fields within the Schumann resonances often match to those of the human brain. The eminent physical neuroscientist, Michael Persinger, and several of his associates have even suggested that there could be information transferring back and forth between the human brain and the Earth's field. This information may be carried in the form of light produced by living organisms known as bio-photons. Indeed such light photons are even emitted from DNA itself.

Kieniewicz leaves us with the question of whether the Earth's field could store human thoughts, just as our brain stores these as memories, allowing other individuals to reach into that field and retrieve them. The next to time you have a strange dream perhaps consider whether it was received from these standing waves, because while in a deep sleep, our brain patterns tend to resonate with the Earth's field making us potentially more susceptible to such information transfer. Might it be possible that we can access the experiences of beings that lived on Earth in the distant past, even those of alien creatures which arrived here hundreds of thousands of years ago?

Another peculiar mode of memory storage is known as *genetic memory*, this concerns memories present at birth that exist in the absence of sensory experience. Ordinarily, such memories become incorporated into the genome over long spans of time. We can think of the programmed automatic behaviour of newborn babies in this category. The emerging field of epigenetics has revealed that life experiences, though not directly coded in human DNA, can be passed on to children. Studies have shown that survivors of traumatic events may have effects in subsequent generations. Our experiences change the way in which genes express themselves, and this genetic expression can then be inherited.

There is growing interest in the capacity for DNA to store memories. That DNA can record many forms of information is no secret, researchers have even come up with a way to encode digital data in DNA. If we were to use DNA to hold our data records, it would provide the highest-density large-scale data storage method ever. Consider that it is calculated we can potentially store around 215 million gigabytes of data per gram of DNA.[5] But what about vivid human memories, can these also be written directly to our DNA molecules?

The famous psychologist, Carl Jung, theorised that we're born with the memories and experiences of our ancestors imprinted into our DNA. This might at first sound a bit hard to swallow, but cutting-edge research is beginning to support Jung's theory. We know today that at least some of the experiences our ancestors went through are providing us with direct knowing today, we call this instinctive behaviour. If specific traumas have passed on warnings to us at an unconscious level, via inherited DNA, might there be far more information stored away that we are just not accessing, or that we are only interacting with at an unconscious level?

Dr Berit Brogaard, a University of Miami philosopher, specialising in the areas of cognitive neuroscience and philosophy of mind, suspects that we may at least be able to tap into specific skills that ancestors had, perhaps a talent for a musical instrument or a gift for mathematics.[6] While Brogaard remains sceptical as to whether we can hope to access fully immersive memories of specific past events, there is an acknowledgement that there is much we do not yet know about the brain. It might be possible that essential memories from our first ancestors can be accessed from our DNA. Not just memories, but also any unique gifts they had – which is a profoundly important considering we are talking about powerfully psychic extraterrestrial beings.

The third scenario has to do with advanced extraterrestrial science. The legendary futurist, Arthur C. Clarke, is known for one quote in particular, "Any sufficiently advanced technology is indistinguishable from magic."[7] We must try to appreciate the difference between technology as we understand it and technology wielded by members of an advanced alien civilisation. Paul Davies, physicist and chair of the SETI: Post-Detection Science and Technology Task group suggests that some extraterrestrial technologies will be non-physical, undetectable or unrecognisable as functional technology.[8] We really do not know the limitations of what highly advanced entities could do to our mental processes remotely.

Evidence of beings far in advance of us, perhaps by millions of years, should include technologies bordering on magical and unthinkable. The peculiar leaf wrapped object that came into Valerie's custodianship might very well be just such a technology, something designed to record events and beam data and images into human minds. It could possibly be that transmissions from the object give recipients the impression of relieving the experiences of the long dead extraterrestrial beings, passing on crucial detailed information by this method. What better way to camouflage an advanced technology on a low-tech planet than to make it look like a rock?

Chapter 4 –Panspermia and the Seeding of Earth

"Our Earth is a living library from other worlds in the cosmos."

We mentioned previously that Alcheringa had explained to Valerie that Earth had been seeded with life by extraterrestrial beings, this happened several billion years before the Pleiadian mothership travelled to the planet. In fact, it was the productive potential of the DNA molecule at the base of all life on our planet, which had drawn the attention of several rather unpleasant species, eventually resulting in them annexing Earth. These rather nasty entities wanted access to the living library of intergalactic genetic codes. The new owners of Earth then used their genetic sciences to create creatures that benefitted them or provided amusement. One of the new species engineered by the invaders was the very first hominin, a distant ancestor of modern humans.

Two scientists from Kazakhstan, Maxim A. Makukov of the Fesenkov Astrophysical Institute and Vladimir I. Shcherbak from the al-Farabi Kazakh National University, have recently publicly claimed that our human species was indeed designed by an advanced alien civilisation. These two scientists should have a good idea of how likely such a thing is, having spent 13 years working for the Human Genome Project – mapping out human DNA.

Makukov and Shcherbak speculate that these alien progenitors either wanted to use our DNA to preserve a complex message or aimed merely to plant life on other planets. They believe that the 97 per cent of non-coding sequences in human DNA is genetic code for alien life forms.[9] This suggestion completely meshes with the information that Alcheringa provided when explaining that our DNA carries the coding for an unknown number of extraterrestrial species. This is precisely what is meant by the description of a living library on Earth recording lifeforms from across the universe. The Human Genome project scientists reached the conclusion that humans were designed by a higher power only after stumbling on a “set of arithmetic patterns and ideographic symbolic language” encoded into our DNA.[10]

This is not the first time that respected scientists have pointed to an alien origin for life on this planet. One of the co-discoverers of the double helix structure of DNA, Francis Crick, found the existence of DNA to be such an unlikely affair, that he suggested it was reasonable to suspect that the first life on Earth was deliberately seeded by an advanced intelligence. The complexity of the DNA code makes it hard to fathom how it could emerge out of some dirt and elementary chemicals swirling about in a primaeval rock pool. Even if we allowed for a vast period to pass, it is debatable whether DNA could spontaneously emerge.[11]

One glaring anomaly is that it did not take life an extensive period to appear on Earth. The planet is calculated to be 4.6 billion years old. Initially, our world was a fireball of magma and hot toxic gases, then around 4.5 billion years ago a thin crust began to form. Incredibly, the first evidence of fossil life has been found in Canadian rock formations dated to 4.2 billion years. The discovery in Canada has led scientists to speculate that life may have emerged on Earth as early as 4.5 billion years ago, almost as soon as there was a crust.[12] It begins to sound like the seeds of life were already in place merely waiting for the right conditions for them to germinate.

The above is precisely the model favoured by Crick and other academics such as Chandra Wickramasinghe, a respected astrobiologist, who have advanced the theory of *panspermia*. For those not familiar with the term, panspermia refers to life on Earth originating from microorganisms or chemical precursors present in outer space. These molecules then spontaneously initiate organic growth once in a suitable environment. Panspermia based models sometimes suggest that the precursors of life might drift through the cosmos inside comets or that they are deliberately sent by advanced civilisations.

In the paper *Directed Panspermia* (1972) Francis Crick remarks, “The time available makes it possible, therefore, that technological societies existed elsewhere in the galaxy even before the formation of the Earth. We should, therefore, consider a new “infective” theory, namely that a primitive form of life was deliberately planted on the Earth by a technologically advanced society on another planet.”

Crick reminds us that the DNA molecule is responsible for all life on this planet, there were not multiple events that gave rise to life on Earth as one would expect if emergence was chaotic and random. If life could potentially happen spontaneously anywhere at any time, why do we instead have evidence that all life began with the same single-celled organisms based on identical DNA strands? Life emerged once only, from there it quickly took root, and that unique process gave rise to all the lifeforms we know to have existed.

There is nothing unreasonable in the idea that intelligent races might choose to seed barren planets, perhaps seeking to terraform them for their later use or to ensure the continuance of their genetic code after a localised extinction event. Equally the dispersal of life across the galaxy might represent a long duration scientific experiment. If that latter suggestion reflects reality, it might also mean extraterrestrial entities would take an interest in the process of evolution as it occurs on planet's they have seeded, perhaps at times visiting to monitor or redirect some part of their experiment. If Earth is a cosmic Petri-dish, it may be that some significant events in our history were directed rather than merely occurring through the workings of chance.

There have been direct discoveries which support the idea aliens are sending the seeds of life out into space, with some of these reaching our planet in more recent times. In early 2015, Dr Milton Wainright, a microbiologist, announced that his team had recovered a minuscule sphere from 16 miles up in the Earth's upper atmosphere, composed of a titanium-vanadium alloy. The tiny object had impacted their sampling device at high speed and was leaking a strange organic goo.[13] It should be noted that vanadium is rarely found in its metallic form in nature and that when used in small amounts with other metals it creates incredibly strong alloys.[14] Wainright tentatively suggested that this object might be a mechanism used by some unknown extraterrestrial species to seed life into the cosmos.

Wickramasinghe and Wainright, are among many scientists that have demonstrated that microorganisms can be carried to Earth by fragmented comets and may potentially give rise to viral outbreaks among human populations. There is already startling evidence that rains of extraterrestrial material from the stratosphere may link to the sudden emergence of new forms of sickness in populations. Whether genetic material from space is directly the cause, or that it provokes mutations in existing viruses remains a matter of some debate. A growing number of scientists are calling for the issue to be taken more seriously.

Professor Edward Steele, biologist and immunologist at the CY O'Connor ERADE Village Foundation in Australia, explains that "Over the past two decades there has been a growing recognition that horizontal gene transfer, via the agency of viruses, might play a key role in evolution. The process of horizontal gene transfer should be extended well outside our planet's biosphere. With current estimates of over 100 billion habitable planets in our galaxy alone, such an extension, admitting the concepts of panspermia would seem entirely reasonable. Over the past decade, there has been growing evidence for microorganisms currently entering the stratosphere of the Earth. Ignoring this possibility of a continuing input of microbial and viral genes to the Earth from the external universe might be fraught with imminent danger."[15]

Viruses and cells have been coevolving with terrestrial organisms since life arose on the planet. Cells evolving to resist their viral invaders can give rise to new forms and behaviours as viruses move genes between unrelated cells, in what scientists call horizontal gene transfer. Horizontal gene transfer explains the presence of genes within organisms that don't come from a direct ancestor, but instead from a separate animal species or some microorganism. This process has played a significant role in creating the tremendous diversity of life on Earth, with virus and bacteria carrying new code into an organism's genomes.[16]

Scientists note that viruses code their genetic information using both RNA and DNA, in single and double-stranded forms. Cellular life uses double-stranded DNA only, this fact led some scientists to suspect that viruses represent descendants of ancient life-forms which lived before DNA existed.

What exactly is it about DNA that supports the theory it probably came to Earth from space rather than having emerged from the chaos of Earths formation?

The DNA molecule is incapable of building itself, it is reliant on proteins. The process for proteins to order correctly is reliant on the information contained within DNA. We have here a molecular process requiring the synthesis of two distinct complex systems, they must emerge together. When we come to consider the mathematical probability of even one single protein arising, things quickly become mind-boggling.

Each protein is constructed from a selection of 20 amino acids, strung together in a precise order to form a chain 200. There is a 1 in 10 to the power of 260 chance of the correct configuration by fortune alone, this number is higher than the total of all atoms in the observable universe. Crick settled on the opinion that it was not feasible that this high level of complexity at the cellular level could have arisen by chance, especially in so short a time span as it did on Earth. This does not mean all life in the universe had the same odds stacked against its emergence, we really don't know if all life is based on the DNA molecule. It might be that organisms emerged first in a very different way and with a distinct foundation, with beings produced from this emergence event later creating the DNA molecule.

It certainly feels unreasonable for such a system to emerge spontaneously when it is reliant on two complex molecular processes and a complex language structure of 4 nucleobases guanine, thymine, cytosine, and adenine combined with 20 amino acids. There also needs to be a translation mechanism, and the proteins themselves are coded in the language of DNA. It also seems counter-intuitive that while life continually evolves, DNA's functionality and the code remained entirely unchanged. The summary here is that DNA appears to emerge improbably fast, is mind-boggling complex, initiated in its perfected form, and remains constant in functionality indefinitely over vast periods of time.

The suggestion that DNA was seeded on Earth would allow for life having emerged over a much more extended period, just not initially on this planet in what is in cosmic or even geological terms, the blink of an eye. Life may have begun with organisms not based on DNA at all, or something else similar, but that DNA has been designed by advanced civilisations as a method to terraform new worlds. The DNA code offers almost infinite possibilities in respect to the organisms it can build and the environments it can shape life towards.

As a lifelong psychic medium and shamanic practitioner, it would be wrong of me to skip over the fact that a significant number of psychics and shamans have also been given the information that Earth was seeded by extra-terrestrial beings. In modern times the American channel, Barbara Marciniak, has written several books in which she shares her understanding that DNA was sent here by entities referred to as 'the planners'. These planners explain to her through psychic communication that the Earth is a living library. This planet stores genetic code for life on Earth including information from a wide range of galactic species – precisely as Alcheringa put it to Valerie.

The famous anthropologist turned shamanic practitioner, Michael Harner, describes a visionary experience he had with the psychedelic potion Ayahuasca, in which he was shown strange dragon-like creatures falling down to Earth from space. These entities informed him they had escaped pursuit by enemies out in the cosmos. The aliens then showed him how they had created life on the early Earth to disguise their presence, hiding within their creations, including within humans. Later, Harner realised that the reference to these creatures hiding within all life might refer to the DNA molecule itself, being that this is inside all organisms. The beings considered themselves masters of the planet and that humans were but receptacles and servants. The communication between them seemed to be coming to him from the lower part of his brain, known as the reptilian brain stem – the most primitive part of the human neurological system.[17]

Harner went on to describe his experience to a respected Conibo shaman, this man recognised the entities described and dismissed their claim over the Earth, clarifying that they were only the "masters of outer darkness" as he pointed up to the sky. Harner had not mentioned the fact the entities had dropped down from space and was considerably freaked out. Later a local evangelist missionary that he spoke to about the visions highlighted the story of Satan's defeat by Archangel Michael, in which it describes a war in heaven after which the dragon and his angels were cast down to Earth, where they went on to deceive the whole world. Harner, as an atheist, was left stunned by the apparent overlaps in the biblical narrative and his experience.

While there is substantial evidence that DNA was seeded on Earth by advanced extraterrestrial civilisations, there is also scientific data which suggests that *Homo sapiens* are not only the distant descendants of spores delivered to this planet but that they were more recently directly engineered from a terrestrial creature by visitors to this world. We will be exploring that evidence in a later chapter. First, we need to understand how extraterrestrial entities might be able to travel to our planet.

Chapter 5 –Warp Drives and Wormholes

"We are moving towards this energy pattern. It is a gateway. The gateway has two spiralling forms, and we are waiting for the right time to move into them."

For extraterrestrial entities to take any role in Earth's prehistory, they would require advanced technologies far beyond anything humans possess today, or at least well beyond anything visible to us in the public theatre. While I can't offer conclusive evidence of how aliens reached Earth, we can at least explore the feasibility of ancient visitations to our planet based on a look at known and theoretical space travel technologies.

My generation grew up in what has been termed the space-age. I was born just a few months after Viking 1 sent the first images of Mars back to Earth, and of course, have lived through a range of subsequent developments including successful artificial probe missions to all the local planetary systems. Until recently humanity has been limited to rocket technology, which has proven inadequate to allow for direct human exploration of the planets in our solar system, the Moon has been our only success story until today.

In just the last couple of years, NASA has been testing a new drive system, known as the EM drive, this has caused a lot of heated debate among physicists as it seems to break the accepted rules by producing thrust without burning fuel. Some calculations suggest that if the EM drive works as hoped it might take astronauts to Mars in as little as 70 days. The Chinese government claims to already have a working prototype of this propulsion system, and other parties are planning their own tests for this new technology.[18]

Scientists are also investigating the potential of Nuclear Thermal and Nuclear Electric Propulsion systems, these could take us to Proxima Centauri (4.24 light years away) in around 1000 years. Compare this capability to the currently utilised electronic ion drive system, using accelerated ions for thrust, which requires an 81,000-year journey to the same star system.

Several theoretical propulsion systems can potentially accelerate our journeys through space, including Nuclear Pulse Propulsion, Fusion Rockets, Fusion Ramjet, Laser Sails, and Antimatter Engines. Unfortunately, for now, all these systems are hindered by a wide range of technical problems. In some cases, we would need an enormous craft with vast reserves of highly specialised fuel, in others the construction costs equal more money than ever available or energy beyond the output of the entire planet. That is not to say they might not be feasible in the future as human technology reaches a far higher level.[19]

There are two theoretical technologies which sound like they might be directly linked to the Pleiadian story. There is a description of how the mothership moves which might suggest something like an *Alcubierre Drive*:

"We don't move into the gateway, we are suddenly just through it. There is no linear movement as such, we are just instantly there."[20]

The Alcubierre Drive is close to the warp drive systems portrayed in the television show *Star Trek*. This technology creates a bubble in the time-space continuum in which the craft sits protected while space is warped to move around it, bringing the destination to the ship rather than the other way around. As the spacecraft is not being propelled forward specific issues concerning time dilation (differences in the passage of time due to velocity) can be avoided. The other interesting point to make is that while the passengers would reach their destination quicker than if travelling at light speed the craft never itself breaks the speed of light (conserving the laws of physics).

This warp drive system would bring two points closer together, at least one source I explored suggested that an Alcubierre Drive would allow a journey to Proxima Centauri in a mere 4 years, other scientists consider that suggestion to be a conservative estimate. Bruce asked for an opinion on this drive system from William Brown, the lead physicist at the *Resonance Science Foundation*.

Fortunately, Brown was willing to offer a detailed summary of the workings and potential capabilities of the warp drive system. In his opinion, there is really no limit to how quickly you can arrive at your destination. Because you are warping both space and time (the space-time continuum), this technology becomes time travel by default. By reducing the distance between two points, there is also a drastic change in the passage of time associated with any voyage, regarding relativity the passengers aboard any craft using Alcubierre drive systems would necessarily be arriving in the past of the destination point (relative to the present time of the departure point). This sounds very strange, because it is, but remember you are not just warping physical space, but space-time, buckling the quantum sub-structure of the universe.

Though there is no doubt that an Alcubierre Drive would be well suited for carrying beings from the Pleiades to Earth, there are some reasons to question if this system was used in the story we are exploring. Both the quotes that I have shared here from Valerie's book refer to a gateway as part of the system which brought the craft to our planet, this strongly suggests a different form of theoretical travel. Brown explains that when you contract space-time beyond a certain degree, this creates a *wormhole*, this is the "ultimate transportation mechanism" because it joins point A to point B. This allows a journey in which there is "no linear movement" and rather than taking any time you are "just instantly there". [21]

What exactly is a wormhole and how could beings travel the universe with them?

Just a little over a century ago, the Austrian physicist, Ludwig Flamm, realised that the equations for the theory of relativity allowed for the existence of 'white holes' a kind of time reversal of black holes. Entrances to either a black or white hole could potentially be connected via a space-time conduit. This solution to the theoretical maths was later further developed by Einstein and physicist named Nathan Rosen. They concluded that there might be bridges between points in space-time, shortcuts for long journeys across the universe, reducing both distance and time taken. This has the additional benefit of reducing time dilation effects associated with extreme velocity, in regular space travel at high speeds time passes much faster for those at the departure point and the destination location than it does for passengers on the rapidly accelerating starship.[22]

This strange theoretical object came to be known as an Einstein-Rosen bridge but is more popularly known as a wormhole. It is necessary for us to accept that Einstein's theory of general relativity mathematically predicts the existence of wormholes. Thankfully, we don’t need to read all the complicated equations for ourselves!

Though no wormhole is currently known by astronomers, it is understood that the entrances would likely be spherical, with a stretched tunnel between them which could be either straight or twisted like a writhing snake. Naturally occurring wormholes would probably be both infinitesimally small and incredibly unstable. Any wormhole useful to space travel would almost certainly need to be artificially created by incredibly advanced technology.

Theoretical physics research suggests that a wormhole containing ‘exotic matter’ could stay open and unchanging for lengthy periods of time. Exotic matter includes negative energy density and tremendous negative pressure, but this type of material has only been indirectly detected in the behaviour of certain vacuum states as part of quantum field theory. Yet, it may be within the capabilities of some alien races to produce quantities of exotic matter for this purpose.

While we can't hope for direct witness accounts from people present on Earth at the time the Pleiadian mothership arrived, there are oral histories and reports of more recent visitations to Earth by beings from the Pleiades. These ancient legends occur in various cultures all around the globe, we will take a quick look at a few examples here.

Wilfred Buck, a science educator of the Opaskwayak Cree Nation, explains that for his tribal group they see a great trickster in the sky when they look up at Orion, this stellar being is pointing towards the Pleiades. The Cree Indians claim that where the Pleiades is positioned there exists a hole in the sky, our planet's connection to the cosmos. It is Buck's opinion that this story refers to an example of the spatial anomaly modern science knows as a wormhole.

In Buck's telling of ancient lore, humans were lowered down from the hole in the sky on a single thread created by mother spider. "We originate from the stars, we are star people,"

Buck says, adding that, "the genesis mythologies say this is where we come from. We come from those stars, we are related to those stars. Once we finish doing what we come here to do, we go back up to those stars."[23]

The Cree are indeed not the only indigenous population that claim an ancestral link to the Pleiades, the same theme is found among cultures spread across the Americas, including the Hopi, Dakota and the Maya. Elsewhere we see the same claims among the Balinese and the Tana Toraja (in Indonesia), the Japanese and the Taiwanese. All the Australian Aboriginal nations have dreaming lore about the Pleiades, many of them tell of a human origin event associated with these stars and seven sisters who came from them to Earth. It is worth pointing out that Australian Aboriginals are the holders of the world's oldest recognised culture and the most deeply rooted oral history. We really do not know just how old some of the Aboriginal dreaming stories are, could they even go back hundreds of thousands of years?

I would really like to briefly mention another connection to this story which appears in the fascinating book series written by the British researcher, Leonard Farra. We have had a personal relationship with Leonard for a little while now, and he has supplied articles for one of our websites and sent us copies of two of his books. He has written a three-book series on his investigation into links between various ancient cultures and the Pleiades. What is perhaps less well known to some of those familiar with his work is that this project was initially inspired by an experience which occurred while he was attending the mediumship circle of the noted British psychic medium, Gerry Sherrick. Some of you may know that Gerry Sherrick was one of the supernatural experts involved with the Enfield poltergeist case which has more recently featured in the plot of a Hollywood blockbuster.

The sessions with Sherrick are described in some detail in Leonard's first book, *Genesis Seven*, he recounts the channelling of a long dead Mexican village elder. This spirit told the group, through Sherrick, that he had lived at a time when seven saucer-like craft landed near his village, many centuries ago. The human-like alien beings that emerged were tall, light-skinned, telepathic and equipped with many advanced technologies. The leader of the visitors informed him that they had arrived from the Pleiades, but it was then clarified that they came from "beyond the time barrier".

There are some overlaps between the descriptions given to Leonard during this session and revelations included in Valerie's book, for example, the mention of a device worn on the forehead which seemed to assist communication which parallels a communication crystal Valerie recalls in the past-life experience, this was worn on her head. More direct relationships are to be found in what these beings left behind before leaving.

The star people told the local leader he would be given a device capable of contacting them. They also informed this person that the seed of the travellers was to be sown in the wombs of the local people's daughters "in order that great leaders would be born" and that this would advance humanity from its present state. The visitors warned the human elder that his people would give birth to children that wouldn't look like members of their tribe and these children would be "high in stature". [24]

You can easily find out more about Leonard Farra's globetrotting investigations in his books, The *Pleiades Legacy: The Stone Age - The Return of the Gods*, *The Pleiades Legacy: The Old World* and *The Pleiades Legacy: The New World*. The information explored above only appears in his now out of print book, *Genesis Seven*. Leonard was so impacted by those first experiences with mediumship that he set out on a lifelong quest for evidence of these purported alien visitations in the ancient past.

When we received a copy of *Genesis Seven*, kindly posted to us by Leonard just a few months ago, I must admit to being left somewhat shocked. There are astonishing overlaps between the information recorded during the Sherrik channelling sessions and things I encountered during my personal time-slips. While Sherrik had retrieved details of the arrival of the Pleiadian time-travellers and their insemination of local women, I had witnessed the aftermath with giant-sized Pleiadean-human hybrids leading the local people. It is hard not to see this as the workings of some higher intelligence, skilfully popping puzzle pieces into place all around me. Such matters as these are not the sort of thing we can call mere coincidence, there is the apparent intelligent ordering of events and arranging the essential connections. Somebody or something is apparently helping me put all this evidence together.

I have to say that it comes as no surprise at all to me that the Pleiadians would have control of a spatial anomaly like a wormhole, not only allowing them instantaneous voyages but also time-travel. On many occasions during my own shamanic journeys to the past, I was given the understanding that the Pleiadians were not only space travellers but also time-travellers. The fact that Sherrik is told these humanoids came from "beyond the time barrier" makes perfect sense in that context.

If you know even just a little about the ancient Mayan culture, you will be aware that they had a bizarre preoccupation with recording and calculating vast spans of time. The Maya not only used several different calendar systems, but these were also used interchangeably to track many different cyclical periods. The famous Long Count Calendar follows a cycle of one *baktun* or 5125 years. It has been noted that five *baktuns* cover 25,630 years, incredibly close to a complete astronomical precession cycle of approximately 26,000 years. This may seem quite an extraordinary interest for an ancient culture, but when you look closer at some of the units of time used by the Maya, things get a whole lot stranger.

Keep in mind that the Mayan culture itself lasted for perhaps two millennia or so, yet they used measurements such as the *Kalabtun* of 157,704-years, the *k'inchiltun* of 3,154,071 years and the *alautun,* an incredible 63,081,429 year-long period. Doesn't it seem just a little bit weird that the low tech early post-Neolithic Maya people needed a word for a period which stretches back to when our mammalian ancestors inherited the Earth from the dinosaurs?

It is not just that there seem to be strange measurement periods, but that in many cases dates engraved on monuments seem to be celebrating events in the future, things which won't happen until several thousand more years have passed. As you zoom in a bit on ancient Maya, it becomes possible to detect the fingerprints of time-travelling beings alongside the normal workings of a megalithic human society. Even the other periods highlighted above have peculiar correspondences, as a Kalabtun covers the period when modern humans emerged from archaic *Homo sapiens*, while a k'inchiltun takes us to around the start of the genus *Homo*. I will leave it there because it would require a separate book to properly explore this subject and my personal experiences with ancient Mayan culture.

I think we have comfortably established links between the indigenous people of the Americas and Pleiadians, as well as to wormholes. Stories around the world claim much the same things. Aboriginal Australians from across their continent have ancient stories about seven sisters from the Pleiades that once visited Earth, often they were also pursued by a hunter associated with Orion. Instead of spiderwebs and cosmic threads coming down to our world, Aboriginal Lore speaks of these beings moving through magical tunnels, climbing magically expanding tree trunks or making use of giant ropes.[25] All these methods for returning to outer space have an uncanny resemblance to what scientists describe as wormholes.

The bottom line is that there is the possibility within known physics that highly technologically advanced aliens might create a wormhole and travel to Earth from a distant star. It is therefore astonishing that ancient cultures describe visitors from space arriving from beyond the time barrier via tunnels, serpent ropes, magical tree trunks and other methods which all sound like laypersons descriptions of just such rifts torn in the fabric of space-time.

Chapter 6 –The Sentient Mothership and Her Tears of Glass

"'Are you aware if pieces of the mothership came to Earth?' 'It sort of melted. There were pieces all around'."

We have already encountered potential extraterrestrial technologies, investigated psychical communications and even travelled through space and time. There is also compelling evidence suggesting that life itself was seeded on Earth. Circumstantial support has been offered for people having witnessed wormholes ripped open in the skies above them. Despite all this persuasive information we have not yet explored solid scientific proofs of this astonishing visitation story. We now understand that any contact event involving extraordinarily advanced extraterrestrial intelligence would be multi-faceted and inherently complex in nature. This feels like the right moment to explore the 'smoking gun' evidence that I am sure you have been looking forward to, it is time for disclosure.

You may remember that the Pleiadean mothership is described as enormous, with a crew count of around 50,000 different beings. This was also not a metal craft resembling human shuttles and rockets, instead it was something more like a huge saucer, grown from a crystalline material. Silicon crystal is well understood to have essential qualities for advanced information technologies, it allows for storage and processing of data when integrated into computer systems. The crystalline structure of the craft enabled a form of consciousness to inhabit the super-structure of the vessel (advanced self-aware intelligence).

We already mentioned in a previous chapter that leading scientists have suggested some advanced extraterrestrial beings might use crystal networks to house high intelligence, so this is something we should expect. This is just the type of technology we should hear about if aliens arrived on Earth!

I would like to briefly refer to a section of the ancient Hebrew religious text known as the *Book of Enoch*. Tradition ascribes this book of Enoch, to the great-grandfather of Noah. You might have already heard ancient astronaut theorists claim that Enoch's writings describe interactions with visiting star beings, during a period before the 'biblical flood'. We can't prove that Enoch met extra-terrestrials, but I think the following highlighted section certainly sounds strangely related to the description of the Pleiadian mothership.

"They elevated me aloft to heaven. I proceeded until I arrived at a wall built with stones of crystal. A vibrating flame surrounded it, which began to strike me with terror. Into this vibrating flame I entered; And drew nigh to a spacious habitation built also with stones of crystal. Its walls too, as well as pavement, were formed with stones of crystal, and crystal likewise was the ground. Its roof had the appearance of agitated stars and flashes of lightning; and among them were cherubim of fire in a stormy sky. A flame burned around its walls; and its portal blazed with fire. When I entered into this dwelling, it was hot as fire and cold as ice. No trace of delight or of life was there. Terror overwhelmed me, and a fearful shaking seized me."[26]

The description offered by Enoch sounds very much like he was carried up into a crystalline vessel, a craft surrounded by powerful energy shields. What are the chances that this obscure text would refer to something sounding so like the details of the already mentioned Pleiadian technologies?

With all these matters considered we need to approach the big question, did a vast sentient crystalline mothership arrive here around 900,000 years ago, only to be destroyed in orbit?

In *ALCHERINGA...when the first ancestors were created*, Valerie offers the understanding that after the mothership, the Rexegena, was destroyed in orbit (around 900,000 years ago) the main body of the ship fell to Earth and became moldavite. There is no doubt that moldavite, a translucent green tektite glass, is a unique material. It is also certainly the result of a massive object falling from space. Moldavite has long been considered a powerful tool for spiritual awakening and is even connected with the legends of the holy grail. If you search the internet, you will find that many websites discuss a possible link between this material and beings from the Pleiades or people that have alien souls (star seeds). I will leave it to the reader to decide where this material fits into this story and I encourage you to hold a piece for yourself and see if it affects you (it also makes lovely jewellery).[27]

Our investigation considered the possibility that moldavite might be the central part of the Pleiadian mothership, but while we do not dismiss it as possible, we can't support this with the current scientific data. Every type of geological dating used concludes that moldavite formed around 14.7 million years ago, as the result of a meteor impact in Southern

Germany.[28] While I do appreciate that an anomalous date might be produced from an examination of material associated with a time-travelling extraterrestrial spaceship this left us with a problem if we wanted to offer objective scientific proofs. However, this initial investigation made it evident to us that moldavite tektite was precisely the type of thing we should be looking for, it being geologically unique, high in silica, non-terrestrial in origin and produced by extreme heat.

Valerie's book had explained that after a double-agent lowered the protective field, the ship was hit by electromagnetic weaponry which shattered and super-heated the hull until it melted. The resulting molten crystalline material which fell to earth could potentially survive for millions of years.

Valerie's book not only provided a good idea of what kind of material I needed to look for, based on the description of the craft and how it was destroyed but also the best region for us to focus our search. The story of the attack includes many smaller saucers fleeing from the enemy attack, with most being destroyed before they get far, others are pursued and blown out of the sky as they attempt to get to the surface. The few survivors apparently landed in Southeast Australia. You will recall that the landing site was near Gosford, a little to the north of Sydney. This is important because between the position of the mothership and Gosford many fleeing saucer ships would have been destroyed meaning debris should fall across that continent. Being able to close in on a reduced target area was massively important, this saved scouring the entire planet for evidence.

There was still a part of me which thought I was on a mission impossible, that there was no way I was going to find the wreckage of an alien craft, especially one blown to bits in outer space hundreds of thousands of years ago. That was all of course only until I found it!

From Southeast Australia spreading towards the northwest, all the way to Southeast Asia is what is today known as the Australasian *tektite strewn-field*. Tektites are a type of glass, it typically forms from a material which has been rapidly heated to the melting point during a high-speed cosmic impact event. Strewn-fields are geographical clusters of tektites, all originating from a shared causal event. As mentioned previously Moldavite is also a glass tektite material.

Tektite glass does not form every time our planet is impacted, in fact, there are only four identified tektite strewn fields despite the many cosmic impact events during geological history. These tektite strewn-fields in order of age are;

North American (34 million years), Central European (14 million years), Ivory Coast (1 million years) and Australasian (0.78 million years).[29] The first three of these strewn fields are associated with identified impact craters, each of considerable size. The oldest of these, the North American strewn-field, is linked to the Chesapeake Bay impact crater, which is over 40km in diameter. Apparently, there is something extraordinary about the fact only four of these strewn-fields exist despite large numbers of asteroids and comets impacting our planet, this immediately makes all of them a little bit strange and anomalous. It would not surprise me if there were alien links to all these debris fields.

The oddity of the tektite subject grows far more significant once you investigate the youngest of these strewn-fields. Australasian tektites are known as australites, and they really are in a division of their own. The first significant fact about australite is that despite being produced recently (in geological terms) and being exceptionally widely dispersed (apparently small related fragments reached over 10% of the Earth's surface), there is no associated crater. This is bizarre as there should logically be a crater which is far more sizable than the one known to be at Chesapeake Bay. The hole sleft behind would also be considerably younger and therefore much more apparent. Scientists suggest the object responsible for all this material should have been around 1 – 2.5km in size and must have hit the planet incredibly hard to cover so much of the globe with debris. So why are there no surface signs of this massive object touching down?[30]

The distribution of australite and lack of source impact site have indeed caused a great deal of head-scratching among geologists. There is a second conundrum which has prompted far more heated debate over the last century, the specific mechanism of australite formation and shaping. Tektites are composed of a rapidly heated material thrown through the air. Initially, tektites are formed from liquid glass. The glass starts to cool during flight, and while partially fluidic the material takes on specific aerodynamic shapes. The pieces are generally hard by the time they land on the ground, but this leaves a problem in the case of australites.

Australite has an additional form which is not known among other tektites, the 'flanged button' which involved a unique double melting process – it is this characteristic we need to explore in a bit more detail. The look of these australite buttons just screams 'we are from space' when you look at them. They look somewhat like small flying saucers, but very much like the re-entry modules from the NASA Apollo program. In fact, NASA scientists analysed australite fragments as a part of their craft design programs, realising the glassy objects offered a unique understanding of the shapes which best suit passing through our atmosphere.

One NASA report has this to say about the nature of the fragments:

"Experiment and analysis indicate that the button-type australites were derived from glassy spheres which entered or re-entered the atmosphere as cold solid bodies; in case of average-size specimens, the entry direction was nearly horizontal and the entry speed between 6.5 and 11.2 km/sec. Terrestrial origin of such spheres is impossible because of extremely high deceleration rates at low altitudes."[31]

The fragments apparently entered at very high speed with flight conditions leading to *deceleration body force* one or two orders of magnitude higher than the earth's gravitational force at the time of impact. While scientists freely admit that nobody knows precisely what the one-kilometre source body was, they do openly acknowledge that it did not have the chemistry of any typical meteorite.

There is only one environment where liquids naturally form spheres and where the temperature is cold enough to freeze molten glass in a mere moment – the vacuum of space. The scientists deduced that the source object for these australite buttons must have become super-heated, melted to a liquid and then pooled into small spheres before the near instantaneous cooling occurred. These glass spheres then rained down through the Earth's atmosphere and began to heat up again, partially melting and allowing unique button forms to be sculpted by the atmospheric resistance.

Researchers of this subject had suggested all kinds of solutions for the source of australites, ranging from a chunk of material blown off the moon or Mars hitting our atmosphere, right through to an asteroid impacting in Southeast Asia and throwing material 60 miles back up back into space, before it rained down again. Every scenario suggested over the last century of investigation has eventually ended without a convincing conclusion, none explained all the associated anomalies.

The single fact agreed upon by all involved in australite research is that the chain of events which created australite was unique in 4.5 billion years. The widely accepted dating for this material places it between 770,000 to 790,000 years in age. Once ever in the history of our planet, just let that fact sink in for a moment. As glaring scientific anomalies go, Australite buttons are a major one.[32]

The composition of individual australite fragments ranges, but they are often up to 80% silica derived from melted quartz crystal. They also contain significant percentages of aluminium combined with around 23 additional elements. I am not a chemist or a geologist so won't speculate on whether the overall composition is in itself highly anomalous, some papers mention it is somewhat unusual in specific percentages of component chemicals and that it is unlike known meteoric material. From what I can understand the elements are all known on our planet, so it is assumed to be the source object was the product of a planetary system with a similar chemical makeup and geological history to Earth.

The only hypothesis that readily explains all the australite anomalies, one which has never been considered, is that the kilometre-wide highly quartz source body was an orbiting extraterrestrial ship exploding at the edge of our atmosphere. The advanced electromagnetic energy weapons vibrated the molecules with a dominant resonant frequency causing the hull to reach enormous temperatures as it fragmented. Parts of the ship became drops of liquid glass; the fluid took spherical form and then rapidly froze in the vacuum to form solid tektite balls. The glass spheres and chunks of the hull entered a deteriorating orbit and began to enter the stratosphere, some parts were accelerated downwards by the final explosion of the mothership's combustible atmosphere.

In my opinion, it is very revealing that most australites are found in Southern Australia, below 25 degrees latitude, this region incorporates the Gosford landing site. This strongly suggests that the main body of the mothership and most of the smaller saucer craft broke up above South Australia. This would explain why the survivors came down in southern Australia, we can imagine some of flying saucers sped directly downwards, indeed at least one of the aircraft is described as crash landing in the waters at Gosford. We can logically guess that those exiting the crumbling parent craft would have headed to the ground as fast as possible to escape the massacre in the skies above and avoid aerial pursuit. If Moldavite was part of this story, it might be that it was a separate section of the vast star-craft, perhaps an internal core composed of a slightly different crystalline material.

Not all australite is in the unique button form so we can infer that more massive chunks of the source vessel broke atmosphere. These more substantial parts would have further fragmented as they came down and become smaller pieces, these would then go through a single phase of melting only. This is precisely what we find, with more usual tektite forms observed for australite found in parts of Australia and beyond.

Many of the tektites found in Southeast Asia are generally considered to be part of the australite strewn-field, these show only single melting and do not include buttons. Scientists are probably correct in thinking that tektites in

Southeast Asia are australites, but I do wonder if they might be instead connected to a separate event which we will be exploring in the next chapter. The most massive pieces of Southeast Asian tektite weigh more than 20 kilograms, known as Muong Nong layered tektites. These large pieces of material are made up of multiple layers of glass that was once molten, there is no well-accepted explanation for this strange layering.

With the incredible weight of some of the Mung-Nong tektites, it is evident that they could not have flown far from an impact site, they are just too heavy, and yet there is no sign of a crater in the local region. The evidence observed seems to fit well with material falling from the sky rather than being displaced by a local impact.[33]

I must admit to feeling slightly sad writing this account, we should remember that tens of thousands of well-intentioned souls perished as the explosion shattered their colony craft. This was also the last moments of existence for the self-aware intelligence inhabiting the crystal ship itself. This was a living being beyond our comprehension, experiencing her death high above an alien world.

I can't help but wonder if the sentient ship felt pain in those final moments, did she perhaps cry?

Chapter 7 –Meteoric Bombardment, Pole Shift and Climate Chaos

"We can pull down a meteor and direct it, some are so big they will shatter a planet. We don't just create tidal waves."

News of the intended betrayal of the Pleiadian colony mission reached the leaders of the alliance council even before the craft had been destroyed. Although the ship was long lost, and little could be done, the second journey to Earth was undertaken, this time it involved a fleet of cosmic enforcers. These ships arrived in orbit around Earth five years after the events already described, and while they did contact the few survivors and offer retrieval, this was not their primary mission. The forces occupying Earth had broken the edicts of the council and destroyed a peaceful mission, there were those who felt there had to be consequences to keep things in order.

These 'space police' were members of a militarised society of feline humanoids, the Leonine race, a species with a long history of combat with the hostile alien race. Although they had conventional weapons in the form of laser type guns, they utilised meteors as their main artillery. Large rocks would be dragged from space using a type of tractor beam technology and could then be launched at specific regions of a planet's surface. This type of planetary bombardment caused immense devastation if needed, a planet could be neutralised efficiently with an extinction level event.

The military force sent a team to the ground and entered the underground realms of the enemy, warning them to return captured technologies and evacuate the planet as initially agreed in their treaty. While many of the residents fled through a wormhole back to their home system in Orion others refused to comply. The military forces engaged the enemy after the failed negotiations and began a bombardment from space involving several large asteroids. Even being underground was not sufficient to entirely evade the aftermath of such an attack.

These descriptions perhaps sound incredible, various strange beings fighting in space above this world and even under its surface. Some aspects of this may yet be impossible to prove, but it seemed to me that there couldn't have been such a cosmic conflagration without leaving some trace? The effect of even a single reasonably sizable meteor smashing into our planet would leave evidence, what then of multiple such hits from all directions?

I felt that such a significant and highly anomalous event should be well-known to scientists, there would have been massive effects on the planet's environment for a long time afterwards, along with craters scarring the surface. I had never heard of anything like that and suspected perhaps there was no evidence of it available, it seemed like something that should be well-known if it had been discovered. Something told me not to give up just yet, after all, if I found any signs of a massive global cataclysm close to 780,000 years ago, it would be hard for anyone to doubt what had already become a very well evidenced narrative. The ship had been located and the fragments dated if one more relevant event could be identified which linked to the revealed date for this mission it would be an incredible achievement.

It took a while to track down, but I eventually discovered there really had been a multiple object bombardment of our planet involving meteors and asteroids, dated to between 770,000 to 790,000 years ago. The reason why this was not common knowledge or anything I had heard about before was that the discovery had only just been announced in late 2016 and then only in one brief news item.

A geological study by a team from Heidelberg University had revealed that multiple meteors all impacted at around the same time, about

780,000 years ago, samples from several sites across Asia, Australia, Canada, Central America and the Darwin crater in Tasmania, all pointed to this same conclusion. The modelling of the event predicted that there would have been massive earthquakes, tsunamis and mass infernos. The chemical analysis indicated that this involved distinct asteroids rather than fragments of a single body and it was clear that they hit the planet from several directions. Beyond the immediate destruction caused, dust and gases would have been thrown up into the atmosphere, blocking sunlight and lowering temperatures. This was a major cataclysm.[34]

There is an interesting article published on Graham Hancock's website written by a Croatian-Italian engineer, Flavio Barbiero, suggesting that if a large enough object hit at the right speed and angle it might change the rotation of the planet. This is called an axial pole shift or earth crust displacement. Barbiero had spent most of his professional life working on research projects for the Italian navy as a specialist in the gyroscopic phenomenon, retiring at the rank of Admiral. He suspected that such a pole shift event may even have moved Antarctica to its present-day location and left a once pleasant land under thick ice.[35]

There is substantial evidence that suggests an axial pole shift event occurred on Venus in the remote past. Venus is the only planet in our solar system both spinning clockwise and entirely opposite to its path around the sun, this is profoundly strange.[36] Scientists have also noticed the planet's rotation is rapidly slowing. Venus already has the slowest rotation of any planetary body in the solar system, so there is no logic behind it rapidly decreasing even further.[37] It looks very much like Venus's crust was once turned right over and that it is now in the process of correcting its direction of rotation. If this could happen on Venus, we must take seriously the possibility that it might also occur on Earth.

Could the aforementioned meteoric bombardment have accidentally, or intentionally, unleashed the horror of an axial pole shift?

It is notable that not long after about 800,000 years ago a shift occurred in the dominant periodicity of glacial oscillations (changes between cold to warm periods) from 41,000 years in length to a 100,000-year period. This is known as the Mid-Pleistocene Transition, and until today nobody understands why it happened. This was a profound and mysterious shift in the well-established climate cycles of our planet. It makes you suspect that something fundamental had changed in respect to the planets rotation, tilt and journey around the sun.

Paleoclimate models reveal that from after 800,000 years ago the global climate became far less predictable and stable, heading into chaos, with wild fluctuations not seen before this time.[38]

As if this were not all entirely enough there is still another enormous change which occurs right on that date of 780,000 years ago, and it's a big one. That just happens to be precisely the timing for the last sudden total magnetic pole shift on our planet. There is some reason to think that this was not an entirely natural occurrence, or that it was part of the other happenings we have been talking about because within the last 20 million years earth had fallen into a pattern of magnetic pole reversals every 200,000 to 300,000 years. The apparent oddity here is that this cycle became disrupted and we are now hundreds of thousands of years overdue another reversal.

The Earth's magnetic field plays a crucial role in protecting the planet from solar and cosmic rays. When the poles switch, this protective shield diminishes to as little as one-tenth of its usual strength. The switching process is thought to take centuries, and during that time radiation would be able to penetrate closer to the ground. Eventually, this radiation could reach the surface of the Earth, rendering some regions uninhabitable and potentially causing localised extinction events for some species.[39]

There is a well-understood relationship between the magnetic fields of our planet and the fields of the sun, these fields interact and provoke corresponding changes. It is considered possible that the magnetic reversals on our world are at least partly triggered by changes in the electromagnetic fields on the sun. Could it be that something strange happened concerning solar output 780,000 years ago?

Today we are in what many people feel is the beginning of a magnetic reversal, the poles are wandering drastically, and the field strength is rapidly decreasing. Geoscientists are expressing considerable concern about the possibility of an imminent total reversal.[40] This would have profound implications for us as a technological civilisation as there would be electromagnetic consequences such as the disabling of satellites and dire effects to the electrical grid. Energy from the sun can potentially enter and cause the collapse of the power system.

The peculiar thing is that we are currently witnessing abnormal solar behaviour. Solar physicists are now saying there are never observed types of activity in the energy dynamics of our nearby star. The number of sunspots has dropped incredibly, even during peaks of the cycle, and this type of drop is linked to sudden violent outbursts. Suffice to say that solar storms thrown our way are a bad thing, overall reductions in activity can also usher in ice-ages.

It has never been established whether the last magnetic reversal at 780,000 years ago was directly harmful to early humans, but as we have already seen it might have been. It is very intriguing that Alcheringa mentions that the star people were suffering a great deal from solar radiation problems on the planet surface. This is most likely just due to their biological and anatomical make-up, but it might also have been connected to the magnetic pole shift or unusual solar activity.

It would be a massive understatement to say that we are stretching the limits of coincidence with so many huge events overlapping in time. We have enigmas piled on anomalies, unique and unexplainable events clustered on a single specific period. Anyone that still feels there is nothing to see here is living in a bubble or has switched their brain to a low power setting. There will of course always be gate-keeper sceptics that merely dismiss everything which does not fit the consensus narratives and the existing paradigms, but we are looking at scientific facts that just don't match the mainstream version of prehistory.

We could probably leave this investigation here and come away with a profoundly changed understanding of the remote past and the foundations of our human epoch. We have seen that this is far more than just the story of star-people visiting Earth, several mega events occurred. This is not the end of our journey though, in fact, it is just the start as we are yet to meet the most important players of all, humans. It is time to take a much closer look at the emergence of the first ancestors of our own *Homo sapiens* species.

Chapter 8 –Our First Ancestors were *Homo Pleiades*

"The star people realise that the only way they can continue as a people on the Earth is to interbreed with an existing species that is able to thrive here. They choose the little hairy ones, a species we ourselves created."

In the accounts provided by Alcheringa and within the many past life memories we are told that after the destruction of the mothership the marooned survivors abandoned the plan to colonise earth. It became evident that without all the advanced technologies onboard the mothership they could not survive for very long in the hostile environment. The group discussed how to move forward and decided that the second-best result would be helping to advance the evolution of the resident hominins and nudging them in a better direction.

It should be mentioned here that the earth hominins had purportedly been engineered from more primitive primates millions of years before the arrival of the Pleiadians. These early human forms had been under the dominance of the hostile extraterrestrial species already on the planet. In normal circumstances, the Pleiadians would probably not have interfered with the development of indigenous beings on a world, knowing the profound impact this would have on regular progression. In the situation of the upstanding-ape, this creature had itself already been artificially engineered and had lived in the presence of an alien race since its beginning. Under these circumstances, there was no guiding principle broken by taking direct action and positively modifying the creature's future potential.

Alcheringa...when the first ancestors were created provides a considerable discussion of the events preceding and involving the first attempts to 'upgrade' the local hominins. With only limited medical and technological equipment it was by no means easy to do. The engineering involved modifications at the genomic level as well as splicing of genetic material from the star-people into the genetic material of the hominins. These 'test-tube-babies' were then implanted into some human mothers and volunteers among the remaining female extra-terrestrials. This process took time to 'perfect', and in the early stages, there were some heartbreaking failures.

This is without a doubt the most important message that we hope to confirm and validate from the material provided by Alcheringa, that humans have a direct ancestry to both primates and advanced beings that came to Earth in remote prehistory. The first ancestor of the *Homo sapiens* lineage was a hybrid creature with both Earth DNA and genes from these Star People. This ancestry makes us a unique organism on this planet. If this statement is factual, we should expect notable anomalous differences separating us from our closest relatives the modern primates.

The ultimate way to identify extraterrestrial DNA in the human genome would be to extract a biological sample and contrast it against another taken from the aliens. We could also potentially identify extraterrestrial genes if we compared the modern human genome to that of early hominins. Unfortunately, we have neither a pure sample of reference DNA from an alien or hominins living before the claimed genetic manipulation. This makes the process of finding the fingerprints of these creator beings considerably more complicated, but not impossible.

We know that all life on earth began with simple single-celled organisms and that over time these evolved toward greater complexity, part of the process involves mutations occurring and accruing over time. My personal view is that mutation only changes members of an existing species while the emergence of entirely new species is a product of specific programs running in the DNA code. The application we know as 'life' runs from DNA code written to produce higher forms of life and increasing complexity (as well as diversity).

It takes considerable time for evolution to create new forms of creatures and for individual difference among members of any species to become apparent. The first thing we should expect if humans have a fundamental difference in the way they emerged is there should be something that makes us look like a relatively new species. If aliens created humans, they would not have the same depth of ancestry that other primates have. Shallow evolutionary history is precisely what we do find, with individual chimpanzees in Africa having more genetic diversity than all seven billion humans across the planet.

Scientists place our split from a common ancestor with chimps at 5-6 million years ago, more than enough time for substantial genetic differences to develop among the members of both lineages, and we would expect these levels to be very much alike. Unlike our closest living genetic relatives, the chimpanzees, all living humans have virtually identical DNA, differing by only 0.1%. This is an oddity, it is almost as though our species lacks the usual depth of ancestry on this planet typical to related mammalian species.[41]

The absence of those genetic differences is our first confirmation that *Homo sapiens* have a strange emergence story. The suggestion that our ancestors were members of a small isolated group that appeared sometime in the last one million years, certainly would help explain the lack of genetic diversity.

Something that I would like to quickly explore is the evidence that at least one group of early hominins had reached Australia before the Pleiadians arrived, although they had craft there is no mention of having to collect humans from elsewhere. Recent archaeology has confirmed that early hominins such as the small hairy *Homo floresiensis* and the taller *Homo erectus* were moving through the Indonesian islands around 1,000,000 years ago.[42] It is considered logical that after crossing the Wallace Line into Flores, the geological divide between Asia and Australasia, these hominins should have easily reached Australia. Further evidence of just such a migration is found in our DNA.

If a small group of early hominins splintered from those across the vast Eurasian continent and moved to Australia, this would cause some initial loss of genetic diversity. A recent study has determined that our ancestors almost halved their biological variety around 1.2 million years ago (+/- 300,000 years).[43] The date range for this event fits very well with the archaeology to the east of the Wallace Line and the suggestion our ancestors were a splinter group isolated in Australia. It is also the case that any small human population isolated in a land with an entirely new ecology would likely undergo uniquely accelerated evolution, even without any external interference.

The next thing we really want to establish is when did *Homo sapiens* start to diverge away from their last hominin ancestor. To understand this, we need to look at some very recent findings. Scientists have extracted DNA from the fossils of Denisovans, Neanderthals and early modern Humans, allowing them to calculate the time these three humans shared a last common ancestor (LCA). This investigation, headed by scientists from the University of Utah, produced a date close to 800,000 years ago for when these three human forms began to diverge.[44]

Several years earlier than the University of Utah research project, a team from the Lawrence Berkeley National Laboratory traced one specific Neanderthal gene's evolutionary history. The team found that the genomic sequence analysed had shared a most recent common ancestor with the reference modern human sequence approximately 770,000 years ago.[45]

There are also beta-globin sequences (a blood protein) in modern Asian populations that are suspected to descend from an archaic hominin ancestor of modern humans living around 800,000 years ago.[46] Without wanting to labour the point, there are multiple lines of evidence pointing to the divergence of the first *Homo sapiens* from the LCA, close to 780,000 years ago.

We can now see that humans have a somewhat anomalous evolutionary beginning and that the timing matches the destruction of the Pleiadian vessel and the many other significant events already explored. The next step in this analysis involves considering the specific differences which separate us from our closest living relatives, the chimpanzees. I am not talking about the noticeable physical differences here, we will talk about those later, right now we want to see if there is anything strange in our genetic makeup.

There is one thing that not only widens the gap between humans and all living primates but also brings us closer to our human cousins the Neanderthals and Denisovans. We are talking about the peculiar fusion of chromosome-2. All primates except for modern humans, Neanderthals, and Denisovans have 48 chromosomes as 24 associated pairs. All living humans today have 23 pairs of chromosomes (other than a few people with chromosomal disorders). Human chromosome-2 exhibits evidence of an end-to-end fusion involving two ancestral chromosomes. The exact mechanism through which these two archaic primate chromosomes evaded their protective *telomeres* (features at the end of chromosomes which prevent fusions) is not yet completely understood. It seems no genes from the end of the ancestral chromosomes 2A and 2B were lost during the fusing.[47]

The fact that Denisovans and Neanderthals share this chromosome fusion with us means it occurred before the divergence of these sub-species, in a shared ancestor.[48] We know this sets the minimum date at close to 780,000 years ago, but we also want information on the maximum age. To find out if the chromosome fusion happened close to the time humans split from Neanderthals or nearer to our divergence from ancestral primates we need to turn to an expert.

I managed to track down the work of Adam Benton, a PhD student of human evolution at the University of Liverpool who had asked a similar question about the fusion of these chromosomes. Fortunately, as an evolutionary scientist, Benton knew what to look for that would narrow down the timing of the event.

The first assumption is that though we have 23 pairs of chromosomes, our primate ancestors would have had 24 pairs, just as do all living primates, this isn't only possible inference as there is visible evidence. Right in the middle of chromosome-2 scientists can see where one chromosome ended and another began. As we explained earlier there is a lack of ancient DNA to compare against from the time when *Homo sapiens* began to emerge, the oldest samples are only around 430,000 years old. This is known to be well after the fusion event occurred.

Lacking ancient reference material, Benton took a straightforward look at the DNA structure itself. First, he explains how things work at that microscopic level. DNA code consists of four nucleotide linked letters, A, C, G and T. These letters are coded in pairs, with C & G naturally pairing, as do A & T. These are not equal pairings as A & T are linked by two hydrogen bonds while C & G have three. This means that C & G have a stronger relationship and that with all else being equal C & G is more likely to replace A & T than the opposite scenario.

However, if a change to C & G breaks a gene this invalidates the additional strength of the bonding, the related mutation is then discarded. In isolated cases around 3% of these substitutions involve swapping of A & T for C & G. When we look at the entire human genome substitution rates equalise. Benton highlights the fact that this bias does occur actively where chromosomes exchange material through recombination, such as the ends of chromosomes.

The fusion site on chromosome-2 displays the bias towards C & G, but today this is no longer being excessively recombined as it is no longer situated at the end of a chromosome. This means it has slightly less C & G than the tips of the chromosome as it has been exempted from this bias for a considerable period. In Benton's calculations, this region has been exempted for approximately 750,000 years, meaning that the fusion can only date to sometime relatively close to that period. We already know the fusion is represented in Neanderthals and Denisovans and that means it occurred a little earlier, at around 780,000 years ago. In simple terms, the fusion of chromosome-2 happed at the time of divergence of the first archaic *Homo sapiens* from their hominin ancestor – no later and no earlier.[49]

With the date of this fusion, event matched you might think we are done, how likely is it that this happened by chance at this pivotal time but unrelated to all the other profound anomalies in prehistory we have explored. It may seem unnecessary to go more in-depth, but this is such a profound revelation and a claim of such great importance that we must establish beyond reasonable doubt that advanced extraterrestrial scientists directed this fusion.

One point that must be addressed is whether the fusion event might have occurred several times among different populations, with *convergent evolution* separately producing similar results. Researchers have determined that all living people have the chromosome fusion at precisely the same site. This lack of variation tells us it only happened once in a shared ancestor, it is not something that ever happened before or after anywhere across the human species.

The next area of investigation concerns the result of the fusion and how it became so prevalent among humans. Some scientists, especially those that believe in the Christian position of *Creationism*, have thrown tough questions at the details of the chromosome-2 fusion event. Dr Robert W. Carter, a biologist, points out that chromosomal fusions, fissions, duplications and rearrangements are most often adverse events for an organism. It is very rare that spontaneous chromosome fusions are neutral, and even less often that they bring any positive changes. Chromosomal fusion is one primary cause of infertility, and indeed most embryos with such a drastic error tend to be spontaneously aborted by the mother's body.

As a rare mutation, the fusion of chromosome-2 should have occurred in just one individual in a single generation, even with the foetus beating the odds and maturing to a live birth this aberration should have soon vanished again, absorbed into a larger population of people with 48 chromosomes. Even if several offspring were produced from two sisters (for example) and all carried the mutation, giving the potential for second-generation couplings where the fusion might be strongly favoured, we would expect at most a small population of people with 46 chromosomes alongside a majority with 48. It is statistically doubtful two children with the same mutation would be produced even by the same parents.

The reality is that as best as can be deduced from evidence, all the earliest ancestors of *Homo sapiens* living 780,000 years ago and onwards had 46 chromosomes. Scientists can't offer a definitive answer to this problem but have made suggestions. One model suggests this fusion event happened within a small isolated ancestral population, allowing it to be spread rapidly across the entire group. A second model posits that perhaps the fusion brought with it some immense benefits that provided an enormous advantage to individuals carrying it. Other scientists think that for the fusion of chromosome-2 to become dominant across the globe in all humans it must have both occurred in a small isolated ancestral population and additionally have provided extraordinary benefits.

This fusion event has the fingerprints of the Pleiadian scientists all over it. The pattern we see matches well with a deliberate scientific experiment involving a group of hominins implanted with modified test-tube babies. There would have been an entire generation of potential breeding pairs born sharing this fusion. It might even be that the aliens themselves carried 46 chromosomes. In one debate I read on a science blog it was also mentioned that there appeared to be a somewhat fortuitous concurrent genic mutation which would have acted to prevent a spontaneous miscarriage of the mutated foetuses!

In many respects the ideal situation would have been to work on a small regionally isolated population, making Australia the perfect setting. Australia has been ecologically isolated from the rest of the world for millions of years, giving rise to a wide range of unique species. I recently heard the famous physicist, Dr Michiu Kaku, talking about the fact that any humans isolated in Australia's unique ecosystem would have experienced accelerated evolutionary adaptations.[50] Such a population would also be cut off from any 'normalising' gene flow from other human communities in Africa, Europe and Asia. For all these reasons it would make it very likely that new mutations would be passed on to the entire local community.

We can't help but wonder what these benefits of the genetic engineering might have been and what did they cause to happen in these new human-alien hybrids. The aim of the project was supposedly creating a superior species, one that would be lifted above all other hominin forms on the planet. We know that this new creature eventually managed to outcompete or absorb all the hominins on earth, that is impressive and further suggests a fantastic upgrade of the species.

Manuel Ruiz Rejón, of Granada University, explains that "...there is a possibility that the chromosome fusion that originated our chromosome-2 may have been associated with the appearance of our distinctive characteristics. Thus, several genes in our chromosome-2 that are found near the area of chromosome fusion are expressed more intensely in our species than in that of large apes. These genes are expressed, above all, in highly significant tissues and organs, such as the brain and the gonads. Secondly, the loss of certain DNA sequences that took place as the result of the fusion may have had 'positive' effects on our ancestors."[51]

The fusion site of chromosome-2 is right in the *intron* of a gene, it is highly unusual for fusions to occur on the intron of functional genes. This makes us wonder which gene is involved and what functions it has. The gene in question is named DDX11L2 and is known to express itself in cells performing tasks related to the nervous system, muscular system, immune system, and reproductive system. Those are some rather crucial areas that an alien scientist might want to influence. The fusion site also contains a DNA sequence known as a transcription factor binding site, this changes how the gene will be expressed. [52]

With the mention of genes associated with Chromosome-2 that relate to the human brain, we can't help but wonder what was done in that respect. Surely any upgrade to a species must involve giving it superior intelligence. It should be considered a red flag for meddling if we can identify sudden beneficial changes in our brain structure around the time of this fusion event. So, do we see any noticeable changes in the human brain around 780,000 years ago?

For several decades evolutionary scientists have been investigating the sudden mysterious acceleration of human brain size which began around 800,000 years ago and continued up until 200,000 years ago.[53] This was a period of unprecedented brain evolution.[54] Before this point in time, our brain size had increased only in harmony with body size. This shift is peculiar in several ways, consider here that a rapidly enlarging brain requires considerable energy to be diverted from other body functions, including muscles. Weakness is probably not a good trade-off for brain growth during a time of creatures fighting tooth and nail to survive.

We also need to appreciate that changes in head size require adaptive modification in the width of the birth canal. The very sudden emergence of significantly larger heads would clash directly with the need for babies to fit through the narrow birth canals of their mothers. This change would undoubtedly lead to a very high mortality rate for both mothers and babies.

When you ponder those negative factors, it becomes evident that a rapidly expanding brain comes with hugely negative implications, it is questionable whether this a good thing for a species in the early generations after the change starts. We will be coming back to these problems later and examining some strange changes in early humans that prevented potential extinction because of the highlighted 'upgrades'.

For the moment let's just focus on a few specific genes which seem to have been part of the modification of the human brain. The first gene of note is called ARHGAP11B, this gene was discovered to be turned on and highly activated in the human neural progenitor cells but wasn't present at all in examined mouse cells. Marta Florio, a molecular and cellular biologist at the Max Planck Institute, explains that this tiny snippet of DNA, just 804 letters long, was once part of a much longer gene. The team were left baffled as to how this fragment had been duplicated, as though a gene had been chopped up and the desired piece copied before being reinserted into the human genome. This is something humans can do today with so-called CRISPR gene editing technologies – but not something we would expect to see occur hundreds of thousands of years ago.

This same gene seems to be uniquely human, it does not appear in primate relatives, but notably, it is found in the genome of both Neanderthals and Denisovans. This tells us the replication and insertion happened before the now well-dated split between these human populations. ARHGAP11B allows the most recently evolved section of the brain, a region called the neocortex, to contain many more neurons. Some scientists suspect this tiny snippet of DNA laid the foundation for the human brain's massive expansion. The human neocortex with its distinctive folds allows for far greater information processing than would a larger brain alone. [55]

Several other genes appear to be unique to humans, separating us from primates, and a number of these relate to our complex brain structure. Another gene, called miR-941, also played a crucial role in human brain development. The gene is highly active in controlling decision-making and enabling language abilities, the study of the gene has caused researchers to speculate that its involvement in advanced higher brain functions is fundamental to making us human.

This gene seemingly emerged fully functional out of non-coding genetic material, DNA that scientists used to refer to as *junk DNA* and in a very brief evolutionary event. While the emergence date has been suggested at 'perhaps one million years ago' we do know it preceded the divergence of Denisovans, as they also carry this gene. Listening to the opinions of one member of the miR-941 research project, Martin Taylor of the University of Edinburgh, we get the impression he sees it occurring alongside the sudden rapid brain growth we already discussed. Taylor explains that the gene, "sprang from nowhere at a time when our species was undergoing dramatic changes..."[56]

Perhaps one of the most famous genes is FOXP2, being that it is closely related to human language abilities. Researchers from MIT and several European universities have shown that the human version of the gene makes it easier to transform new experiences into routine procedures. Neuroscientists have found that mutations in this gene have occurred several times in the last 500,000 years, playing a significant role in our ability to produce and understand speech. Perhaps less well known is the fact that the initial version of the FOXP2 transcriptional factor, which enhanced synaptic connectivity and malleability in neural circuits, is also shared with Neanderthals, and Denisovans.[57] It seems clear that our extraterrestrial benefactors wanted us to be able to talk to each other.

Chapter 9 –Children of Earth

"Many of us had been artificially impregnated with our own seed that had been genetically modified to produce a new being, able to cope with the sun and atmosphere of this place. More important, the newborn would be of the light."

Creating an 'upgraded' human species with higher brain capacity would inevitably involve some enormous challenges, one of the most immediate is how do you get a significantly larger head to fit through the existing narrow birth canal. If all the next generation of babies cause their mothers to die in childbirth, likely expiring along with them, the experiment would immediately end in an extinction event. It appears that the alien scientists came up with an ingenious workaround for this problem, they modified the growth cycle of the foetus so that birth would occur before the full development of the infant happened.

The majority of mammal foetus develop to a high degree of maturity in the womb before birth. This provides the advantage of young animals being able to reach a reasonable level of self-sufficiency in a remarkably short time following delivery. We can see that a great many mammals produce young able to walk within hours of birth, within a few weeks they are able to supplement mothers milk with the food they forage for themselves. Mobility also allows young animals to potentially evade predators or flee from other dangers.

If we look at horses, for example, we can see that a foal walks almost immediately, it grows to its near adult height and size (around 80% of this) within a year or so and then enters puberty by around two years of age. After about four years the foal is an adult horse and will likely live into its twenties, all being well. Things could not be more different with human babies and the development stages the pass through.

Human infants are born while still in their foetal stages of development, we can observe this in the fact the bones of the skull have not yet fused and in the lack of spinal strength, they can't even safely support the weight of their own heads. Our offspring are incredibly dependant on their mothers for sustenance, initially continuing sole reliance on nutrients from the mother's body for a further six months. It takes about the same time, six months, for the neck muscles to become sufficiently strong, also for the first attempts at crawling to begin. All this while the human brain growth continues at an incredibly rapid pace. If we return to our foal for a moment, we can expect to see it walk or run within a few hours of birth.

Being born as a foetus allows our species to have a lengthy period of rapid brain expansion beyond the womb, sparing mother's additional pain or extremely high chances of death during childbirth. We also have substantially elongated infancy, walking takes around 18 months to unfold, and speech typically begins at approximately two years of age, concurrent with the fusing of the bones of the skull. This might be the end of our foetal stage, in which we are astonishingly vulnerable and fragile, but it only opens into an incredibly long stretch of childhood with continued parental dependency.

While every child is slightly different, no child will be physically mature or capable of sexual reproduction, until somewhere between 10 to 16 years of age. Within this same period, many of our fellow mammals have completed their entire life cycles or will be heading into their senior years of physical decline. Even after all these years have passed a human is not fully developed either physically or psychologically, they are however at least finally capable of keeping themselves alive.

Humans are what they are today primarily because of this greatly elongated maturation period, the correct term for this stretched childhood is *neoteny*. I imagine many readers probably haven't heard of neoteny as it is not a widely discussed subject outside of academic circles. It is related to the better-known term neonatal, of course, and is all about infant development – or more specifically the retention of juvenile features in an adult animal and the sexual maturity of an animal while it is still in a mainly larval state. The term *pedogenesis* also refers to this phenomenon.

Perhaps the best-known example of a highly neotenic creature is the Mexican axolotl. The axolotl is essentially a larval salamander which can breed while still in its juvenile form and does not usually ever mature into the adult body type. While the axolotl looks physically very different to salamanders, at the DNA level, they are identical. Scientists have discovered that larval salamanders require iodine to trigger maturation, in the region where the axolotl lives there is a lack of iodine in the pools in which the young are hatched. It appears that at some time in the past some of the young creatures adapted to their problematic environments through becoming fertile without ever becoming a land-dwelling salamander. Some axolotls, a tiny minority, eventually crawl out of their pools and become adults.

One common reason why a great many people have a knee-jerk dismissal reaction when they are told modern humans evolved from an ape-like primate, is that we just look so incredibly different from living primates. The physical, morphological, differences are then added to the extreme behavioural differences between apes and humans. There is a sense of us being a wildly different species. The truth is that there are both extremely close links between all primates, including us, and yet also some profound differences.

It is often said that we share almost 99% of our DNA with chimps, in one sense this is true, but it really depends on how you contrast the genomes of the two species. When we look at the various mutations, segment repeats, section omissions and which genes are currently expressing or turned off, that high figure can be revised downwards quite considerably. Where it really counts, in genetic expression, humans have some genuinely profound differences from chimps. So, what about our unique looks?

Once we move beyond primary anatomical overlaps, humans look very unlike chimpanzees, we can all plainly see this with our own eyes. If we are fellow primates, essentially an unusually large-brained form of bipedal ape, why do we look so different?

The answer to how modern humans acquired their strange appearance can be found in an exploration of the neotenic process. Look again at chimpanzees, specifically the head profile of infant chimps, the resemblance to a human child is stunning. Some of our features, including a disproportionately large head, rounded skull, flat face, lack of thick body hair, and several other traits, are shared between humans and infant chimpanzees. It becomes clear that we are something like the axolotl, human beings are an ape stuck in its infant form throughout life.

We can even see that our face is now flatter than it once was because we grow too many teeth for the size of our jaw. Most people do not have straight teeth and a great many need to have teeth removed to allow for others to grow straight. This is because we have lost the protruding lower jaw typical of adult apes. Evolution of the mouth has not yet caught up with the sudden flattening of our face.

Significant neoteny in humans began around the time that the first members of our genus, *Homo*, emerged, sometime between 2 -3 million years ago.[58] This initial progression in neoteny increased the maturation period and allowed for the size of the human brain to expand, even if only gradually. We might recall that the Pleiadians have told us the first archaic humans were created by a rival extraterrestrial species, it is likely this first neotenic shift was related to initial engineering of the *Homo* genus.

Academics have found that at the start of the *Homo genus* there was an incomplete segmental duplication of the ancestral gene SRGAP2. This event produced a new gene, SRGAC2, which slowed spine maturation and allowed for more neuronal migration. The new gene had a drastic effect on dendrite spines, anatomical substrate involved in memory storage and synaptic transmission, perhaps also increasing potential contacts between neurons in the brain. The mutation resulted in higher synaptic densities in humans when compared to other primates.

Scientists involved with studying SRGAC2 found that around 48% of the genes involved in the development of the prefrontal cortex changes differently in humans and chimpanzees during the ageing process. The summary offered in one academic paper is that a "significant excess of genes" related to the development of the prefrontal cortex show "neotenic expression in humans" relative to chimpanzees. The notable contrast between these species is best explained by the neoteny hypothesis of human evolution, that we are primarily a neotenic ape. [59]

The Pleiadians were aiming much higher than the creation of a simple-minded servile hominin species, and as such, they drastically accelerated the ongoing process of neoteny in humans. Not only was this required to allow us our larger brains, without dying in childbirth, but would fundamentally change how we behaved, thought and communicated. It is worth mentioning that the retention of the fine body hairs typical of a late stage ape's foetus would enable humans to rapidly lose excess heat. Overheating is a potential problem for large-brained creatures as brains burn a lot of calories for neural processes.

Neoteny also had implications for the psychological make-up of humans. Infants have more cognitive flexibility, they learn many new skills concurrently, use abstract thinking and have beautiful leaps of imagination. The brain of a child is hard-wired towards curiosity, prompts a thirst for learning and has powerful information absorption capabilities. The neural networks are very plastic and flexible while we are young, continually rewiring to suit new tasks. Infants specialise in replicating observed behaviour, they must if they are to mature. One distinct characteristic of young animals is the desire to play, extreme playfulness can be observed in the offspring of almost any mammalian species.

Adult animals typically become very stuck in their ways, they specialise in a skill-set and then fixate on repeating a small number of essential activities. Adults across the animal kingdom are generally not very interested in play, instead focussing almost exclusively on home building, finding mates, raising young and foraging for food. By retaining a child-like brain structure into adulthood, humans became perhaps the most mentally flexible and environmentally adaptive species on Earth. Many typical adult human psychological characteristics such as our incredible curiosity, playfulness, overt displays of affection and indeed much of our complex social behaviour, are products of neoteny.

There were also substantial social implications that accompanied increased neoteny. In a species where infants can walk and gather food soon after birth, there is less requirement for adults to dedicate time and energy to child rearing. Producing highly independent young reduces the need for an adult to engage in communal living or utilise complex social behaviour – moving in groups is merely a way to increase protection from predators and improves the chances of locating food sources.

The lengthy total dependence of human infants on their mothers and their incredible vulnerability make it almost impossible for them to survive to adulthood without help from an extended family grouping. If we imagine a lone mother with her baby having to gather enough food for milk production over many months, while continually holding that baby, it becomes apparent this would be incredibly impractical. This mother would also need to defend herself and her infant against opportunistic predators.

Humans are relatively weak, they have no horns, claws or long fangs. There are very few large predatory animals that humans can defeat in one-on-one unarmed combat.

A mother with a baby is both vulnerable and hindered in gathering food, she needs at least a mate who dedicates himself to helping her. The survival of a human child really requires the efforts of a large group in which food is communally sourced, resources shared, and many adult carers available. It is quite clear that our early ancestors would not have flourished as a species without communities.

In many respects neoteny represented the spark which led to human communities, any sane mother wants her offspring to survive and will do what is best towards that aim. The best thing for a mother is then to find a partner with the same dedication, maintain close relationships with immediate family members and form social contracts of mutual support with other adults. In fact, we now know that much of our sizeable complex brain is dedicated to processing information about other humans, there is considerable value in knowing about other people, and how to best maintain an optimal position within a highly complicated group structure. Essentially our brains are hard-wired for gossiping and social networking – no surprise then that even today most humans love both activities!

Evolutionary scientists have also deduced that many neotenous traits have been highly favoured in mate selection. Women today have more neotenous features than males, we typically have less body hair, smaller noses, larger eyes, flatter faces and delicate jawlines. These and other child-like features have evidently attracted male partners and caused these traits to be reinforced, in fact, studies have shown men to prefer women with greater neoteny.

Many typically neotenic features are found to be favoured above those we often associate with sexual attraction such as shapely bottoms and breasts. Consider that even a woman with an hourglass figure, long legs, large pert breasts and luscious long hair will still struggle to find an ideal mate if she grows chest hair, a full moustache and sports a prominent brow ridge or protruding square jaw. Adult ape features such as these described are not considered desirable in human females.

It is suspected that men's natural programming to help and protect children meant they tended to extend this more often to women with child-like features. Women would have selected men that had an active protective urge towards children, this strongly reinforced these traits in males. We can easily see how this creates a feedback loop and ensures that most successful interbreeding involves women with greater neoteny and their genes will favour children (both female and male) which the same neotenic features.[60]

The process of increasing neoteny is also observed in some other species, especially domesticated animals. This is very intriguing because once our wild ancestors were taken into the genetic engineering and breeding program, they were being tamed by the alien scientists. These long-lived visitors to our planet were able to ensure several generations of interbreeding favoured traits they wanted to bring out while avoiding any problematic inbreeding. This is very much how we have shaped animals such as dogs over many generations of deliberate directing of bloodlines.[61]

It seems likely that once direct shepherding came to an end, perhaps as the human population size expanded beyond the limits of such influence, a process of self-domestication took over. The preference for partners with a pro-social outlook would have ensured ongoing taming of human nature. The Pleiadians may have started this ball rolling, but we have kicked it all the way down the road.

"One reason that made scientists claim that humans are self-domesticated lies within our behavior: modern humans are docile and tolerant, like domesticated species, our cooperative abilities and pro-social behaviour are key features of our modern cognition," says Professor Cedric Boeckx. "The second reason is that modern humans, when compared to Neanderthals, present a more gracile phenotype that resembles the one seen in domesticates when compared to their wild-type cousins," added Boeckx. [62]

While some recent studies have found that there is a statistically significant number of genes associated with domestication that overlap between modern humans and various domesticated animals, intriguingly this genetic overlap was not observed concerning Neanderthals. When we look at Neanderthals, it is clear they have fewer neotenous features than modern human populations. It appears that Neanderthals went feral at some stage in prehistory, they fragmented into small isolated family groups and lived wild, rugged lives. In taking a less domesticated path Neanderthal morphology changed, the indefinite childhood was lost, and they started to grow up and become adult-form humans (more ape-like).

It seems that what really separates these two human groups is not so much genetic divergence as behavioural changes. Due to epigenetic effects, Neanderthal choices began to impact gene expression. As our cousins abandoned complex social behaviour, this reversed the some of the associated neotenic changes. It seems we really are quite literally the product of our thinking and actions. Every action we take right now, every idea we have is shaping not only ourselves but our descendants. We better decide now what we want humans to be in the future!

It is abundantly clear that the visitors from the Pleiades always intended for humanity to have the ability to choose their own destiny, forge their future and shape themselves. It is in our DNA, written in the code. Neanderthals eventually returned to the wild places and lived a less socially complex lifestyle with just their extended families. Modern humans have gone down a different path, one which has led to increased social networking and human interconnectivity, this choice has brought us to a moment of incredible possibility.

Our technological development will take us out to the stars in the not distant future. It seems this is a feat that other beings achieved an aeon ago, allowing them to visit this world. Perhaps they always hoped some of us would one day look up and sense them out there in the void and be drawn to meet them on more equal terms. What should also be clear from this research project is that they have never completely turned away from this world, instead retaining a constant, even if limited, level of contact. This relationship has remained in place the entire time our species has existed.

Modern humans have evolved to be freethinkers, artists, multi-taskers, friends and to dance beneath the stars. This is precisely how most indigenous people have lived for millennia, in close relationships with each other, with their land, animal life, spirits and star visitors. Those of us in developed nations see this way of life being rapidly taken away from us, with social structures that are crushing abstract thinking, limiting people to intense specialisation and promoting one job for life modalities. There are even punishments for those that think outside the box or offer views counter to orthodoxy.

Acceptance of spirits, star people and even our profound intuitive gifts are ridiculed by those that own and control our media and education systems. There is something very wrong here, we seem to be heading back into the prison-like situation the Pleiadians rescued us from almost 800,000 years ago. I can't help but ask if that is because humans want to take that direction or if there is some external interference?

Now that we know we were never alone, we must ask, who else is walking with us? Doesn't it feel like there has always been a hidden hand trying to derail the optimal path for our species? Who benefits from the destruction of our ecosystems and the near-enslavement of vast numbers of people in the developing world?

You might be wondering if there are people that already know the truth of our origins, perhaps those in the secretive intelligence community, government officials or scientists in secret research projects. Could there be people already in possession of this knowledge and using it against the rest of us to their advantage?

Obviously, I do not have top secret clearance, but there is something to consider here. On April 9th, 1983, investigative journalist, Linda Moulton Howe was in a meeting with US air force intelligence officer Sgt Richard Doty. Doty handed a file to her with the heading 'Briefing for the President of the United States on the Subject of Unidentified Aerial Vehicles'. The document was lengthy, but two lines leapt out for Moulton Howe, one that said, 'Extra-terrestrials had manipulated DNA in an already evolving primate species to create *Homo sapiens*'. Another line clarified that something called *Project Garnet* had successfully answered all questions and mysteries about the evolution of *Homo sapiens* on this planet.[63]

Hearing this astonishing information which dates to the early 1980's certainly gives us some food for thought. Perhaps what seems like revolutionary knowledge on the existence of advanced alien life, and the role it has played in human origins is old news to elite members of our planet's increasingly draconian power structures.

Contact has begun; indeed, we are deep into the process, the only question remaining to be asked is whether our species is ready to take this relationship to its next logical level?

Conclusion

"The Earth will soon enter into a new golden age, one of love and peace. On that day there will come a final choice. Some people have spoken of it as 'The Judgement Day'. This is correct, but it is a judgement of the self by the self."

At the very start of this journey, I mentioned that New Scientist magazine listed the most significant questions people ask, with the top choice being, what is reality?

While it is true that we have not explicitly investigated the nature of reality, it is also apparent that we have inadvertently covered a great deal of material relevant to that subject. The Pleiadians are apparently quite able to bend the space-time continuum as though it were nothing more than a rubber sheet. They have no problem uploading consciousness into a crystal spaceship or creating self-aware recording and communication technologies which look like nothing more than an ordinary stone.

For these cosmic beings, it seems that planning events across a stretch of hundreds of thousands of years are hardly more of a chore than were we arranging an outing on a long summer's day. Perhaps most astonishing of all these extraterrestrial entities seem to be able to download their consciousness into humans, dolphins, birds or even other alien beings with less trouble than we might have to get our pants on in the morning. We can certainly understand why their visits during prehistory might have led to some stories of sky gods. Underlying all this strangeness is the simple message that in respect to the fundamental nature of reality, all is not quite as it seems. The mundane background existence that we consider to be firmly fixed in place appears to be far more plastic and malleable than we ever imagined.

Even with all our great achievements and remarkable technologies, the nature of the Pleiadian contact with Earth that we have explored, and the things they have shown us, immediately call to mind that line from Randy Bachman's classic rock song, "you ain't seen nothing yet."

It is my opinion that the Pleiadians have always wanted humanity to reach a point where there is a request from us for them to engage in open, transparent, full communication with everyone on this planet. They have remained engaged with humans through psychic interactions and seemingly at least some face-to-face visits with selected contactees. More than that it is abundantly clear to me that there are people on earth housing souls that once inhabited Pleiadian bodies, people known as *starseeds*.

It has been demonstrated that the Pleiadians would like our species to progress and improve, but one does wonder what they make of our current situation. We live in a time when vast numbers of people are left to starve while enormous sums are spent on weaponry, much of it later used to mass-murder innocent civilians. We are led by the worst humans available, serial liars, greedy fraudsters and outright psychopaths and perhaps worst of all the population does not appear to be doing a great deal about changing this situation.

It may seem to observers from beyond that humans are nowhere near ready to join a galactic community incorporating assorted advanced intelligence. Indeed, one might wonder if some of the beings up in space are not tempted to wipe the slate clean with another one of those cosmic bombardments we explored earlier, humans do not seem to have done better with the planet than the unpleasant beings the Pleiadians removed.

The word Alcheringa can be understood to mean the time in which the first ancestors were created, but it can also mean 'the golden age'.

Many ancient stories tell of cycles on our planet involving periods of high spiritual development, in which master teachers existed, and humanity lived in harmony. These periods are most often called golden ages, but we should also understand that many of these times came to an end with incredible cataclysms, almost always associated with human behaviour falling to an all-time low. That is not to say all are punished equally, these myths and legends make it clear specific civilisations or cultures bear the brunt of these troubling cleansing events. Those meriting a second chance are saved and take on the challenge of building the new global civilisation. It reminds us of that famous line from the Bible, "Blessed are the meek, for they shall inherit the earth."

I do not want to sound overly dramatic but knowing that we are not alone is a double-edged sword. On the one hand, we seem to have the possibility of joining a galactic community of advanced beings. On the other hand, we are being watched by powerful entities that don't seem to tolerate extreme abuses of power, slavery and the enabling of evil. There is also the fact that we are told this world is an essential living library of galactic genes. Our ongoing man-made extinction of life-forms and the devastation of the environment might not sit well with intergalactic civilisations. We may be burning the contents of their galactic library.

I hope that this book offers, firstly, a solid presentation of evidence which validates the existence of extraterrestrial beings. Beyond that my wish is for it to become a call to action, we really are at a momentous fork in the road. We are right on this cusp of a significant transition. We are almost an intelligent species, very nearly recognisable as 'highly technological' and even 'space-faring'. This is a moment which is no doubt exciting for any extraterrestrial groups that are interested in our world, and I imagine most are cheering us on in the hope that we make a successful transition. Probably they at least hope we don't blow ourselves back into the stone age or don't need them to step in and redirect our actions.

There is a reason this book has only become possible to write now and at no time before, that these beings have brought about the situation where this book can exist right now. This is a message, this is contact, but it is both an invitation and a warning. The question is, what will we do next, what is our response?

Help Change the Paradigm

I hope that this book has been an enjoyable and mind-expanding journey for you and will leave you with food for thought. If you feel that this is a book that other people should read, please take just a couple of moments to leave a short review on the Amazon page. Every review really helps the book reach somebody else that might gain from reading it.

With your help, this book will help to change the way humanity thinks about the extraterrestrial subject and the human origins story. Let's move disclosure one step closer.

References

[1] Spencer, B & Gillen F. J., 1899, The Native Tribes of North Central Australia
http://www.sacred-texts.com/aus/ntca/ntca06.htm

[2] Schneider, S., 2014, Alien Minds Chapter 12
http://www.datascienceassn.org/sites/default/files/Alien%20Minds%20-%20Susan%20Schneider.pdf

[3] Thames, F, 2016, New Year's Eve With(out) Arthur Guirdham
https://ellisctaylor.com/2016/01/09/new-years-eve-without-arthur-guirdham/

[4] Kieniewicz, P, 2015, How Private are our Thoughts?
https://explore.scimednet.org/index.php/2015/10/01/how-private-are-our-thoughts/

[5] Service, R. F., 2017, DNA could store all of the world's data in one room
http://www.sciencemag.org/news/2017/03/dna-could-store-all-worlds-data-one-room

[6] Dr Berit Brogaard, 2016, Can We Access the Memories of Our Ancestors Through Our DNA?
https://www.vice.com/en_au/article/ypv58j/genetic-memory

[7] Clarke, A. C., 1962, Hazards of Prophecy: The Failure of Imagination

[8] Davies, P., 2017, The Alien Observatory --"Advanced Life May Exist in a Form That's Beyond Matter"

http://www.dailygalaxy.com/my_weblog/2017/09/-the-alien-observatory-advanced-life-may-exist-in-a-form-thats-beyond-matter.html

[9] DiscoveryCSC, 2013, In the Planetary Science Journal Icarus, the "Wow!" Signal of Intelligent Design https://evolutionnews.org/2013/03/a_wow_signal_of/

[10] McKanzie, C, 2017, Mystery Of Our Coded DNA – Who Was The 'Programmer'? http://www.messagetoeagle.com/mystery-of-our-coded-dna-who-was-the-programmer/

[11] Directed Panspermia Hypothesis http://www.panspermia-theory.com/panspermia-theories/directed-panspermia

[12] Ghose, T, 2017, World's Oldest Fossils Possibly Uncovered in Canada https://www.livescience.com/58065-evidence-of-ancient-life-unearthed.html

[13] Speigel, L, 2015, UK Scientists: Aliens May Have Sent Space Seeds To Create Life On Earth https://www.huffingtonpost.com.au/entry/aliens-send-space-seed-to-earth_n_6608582

[14] Gomes, H. L. & Baxter, H. A., 2016, Vanadium: the 'beautiful metal' that stores energy https://theconversation.com/vanadium-the-beautiful-metal-that-stores-energy-57775

[15] Wickramasinghe, N. C. & Steele E. J., 2016, Dangers of Adhering to an Obsolete Paradigm: Could Zika Virus Lead to a Reversal of Human Evolution? https://www.researchgate.net/publication/304505032_Dangers_of_Adhering_to_an_Obsolete_Paradigm_Could_Zika_Virus_Lead_to_a_Reversal_of_Human_Evolution

[16] Tasoff, H, 2018, Interstellar Influenza? Space Viruses Could Reveal Alien Life https://www.eurekalert.org/pub_releases/2018-01/psu-vae011818.php

[17] Harner, M, 1992, The Way of The Shaman, pp. 3-5 https://acausalrealms.wordpress.com/michael-harners-ayahuasca-experience/

[18] Waugh, R, 2017, China Claims They Have Actually Created an EM Drive https://futurism.com/china-claims-they-have-actually-created-an-em-drive/

[19] Christoforou, P., 2016, How Long Would a Spacecraft Take to Reach Proxima Centauri? https://www.astronomytrek.com/how-long-would-a-spacecraft-take-to-reach-proxima-centauri/

[20] Barrow, V., 2002, Alcheringa...when the first ancestors were created

[21] Brown, W., Personal correspondence

[22] Redd, N. T., 2017, What is a Wormhole? https://www.space.com/20881-wormholes.html

[23] Buck, W., 2016, Cree mythology written in the stars http://www.cbc.ca/radio/unreserved/from-star-wars-to-stargazing-1.3402216/cree-mythology-written-in-the-stars-1.3402227

[24] Farra, L., 1987, Genesis 7, pp. 5-9

[25] Seven Sisters http://www.kitezh.com/sevensisters/7sisters.htm

[26] Book of Enoch, Chapter 14:10-12 http://www.sacred-texts.com/bib/boe/

[27] Barrow, V., The Moldavite Story A green crystal – known as the Moldavite Stone
http://www.valeriebarrow.com/?p=48

[28] Frantisek, 2014, Tektites dating – determining the age of moldavites
https://www.aboutmoldavites.com/tektites-dating-moldavite-age/

[29] Fry, C., 2013, Known tektite strewn fields and finds
https://www.researchgate.net/figure/Known-tektite-strewn-fields-and-finds-from-McCall-2005_fig2_290391882

[30] Massive Missing Meteorite Impact Crater Hunt Narrows After Glassy Debris Uncovered In Antarctica
http://www.iflscience.com/environment/massive-missing-meteor-impact-crater-hunt-narrows-after-glassy-debris-uncovered-in-antarctica/all/

[31] Adams, E. W. & Huffaker, R. M, 1962, Aerodynamic Analysis of Tektites and Their Parent Bodies
https://ntrs.nasa.gov/search.jsp?R=19980223611

[32] Tektites (Australites)
http://earthsci.org/space/space/tektites/tektites.html

[33] Fiske, P. S. et al., 1999, Layered tektites of southeast Asia: Field studies in central Laos and Vietnam
https://onlinelibrary.wiley.com/doi/pdf/10.1111/j.1945-5100.1999.tb01388.x

[34] Martin, S., 2016, Multiple meteors hit Earth causing devastation including tsunamis and huge earthquakes
https://www.express.co.uk/news/science/646779/Multiple-meteors-hit-Earth-at-same-time-causing-widespread-devastation

[35] Barbiero, S., 2006, On the Possibility of Instantaneous Shifts of the Poles

https://grahamhancock.com/barbierof1/

36 Franzen, H., 2001, Why Venus Spins the Wrong Way https://www.scientificamerican.com/article/why-venus-spins-the-wrong/

37 Major, J., 2012, Venus Spinning Slower Than Thought—Scientists Stumped https://news.nationalgeographic.com/news/2012/02/120214-venus-planets-slower-spin-esa-space-science/

38 Chalk, T. B., 2017, Causes of ice age intensification across the Mid-Pleistocene Transition http://www.pnas.org/content/114/50/13114

39 Worral, S., 2018, Earth's Poles Will Eventually Flip, So What Then? https://news.nationalgeographic.com/2018/02/earth-magnetic-field-flip-poles-spinning-magnet-alanna-mitchell/

40 Pappas, S., 2018, An Electro-Blob Under Africa May Be 'Ground Zero' for Earth's Magnetic Field Reversal https://www.livescience.com/61958-africa-blob-earth-magnetic-flip.html

41 Genetics and Human Health: A Primer https://www.alrc.gov.au/publications/2-genetics-and-human-health-primer/genetic-difference-genotype-and-phenotype

42 Moore, M., 2016, How the Hobbits kept their tools as they shrank into island life https://theconversation.com/how-the-hobbits-kept-their-tools-as-they-shrank-into-island-life-59529

43 Akst, J., 2010, Ancient humans more diverse? https://www.the-scientist.com/?articles.view/articleNo/27922/title/Ancient-humans-more-diverse-/

[44] Huff, C. D., 2017, New Look at Archaic DNA Rewrites Human Evolution Story https://unews.utah.edu/new-look-at-archaic-dna-rewrites-human-evolution-story/

[45] Noonan, J. P. et al., Sequencing and analysis of Neanderthal genomic DNA https://www.osti.gov/servlets/purl/923281

[46] Harding, R. M. et al., 1997, Archaic African and Asian lineages in the genetic ancestry of modern humans. https://www.ncbi.nlm.nih.gov/pmc/articles/PMC1712470/

[47] IJdo, J. W., 1991, Origin of human chromosome 2: an ancestral telomere-telomere fusion. https://www.ncbi.nlm.nih.gov/pmc/articles/PMC52649/

[48] Venema, D., 2012, Denisovans, Humans and the Chromosome 2 Fusion https://biologos.org/blogs/dennis-venema-letters-to-the-duchess/denisovans-humans-and-the-chromosome-2-fusion

[49] Benton, A., 2016, Adam's chromosomes were fused (and he lived earlier than we thought) http://www.filthymonkeymen.com/2016/11/08/adams-chromosomal-fusion/

[50] Kaku, M., 2016, Mankind Has Stopped Evolving http://bigthink.com/dr-kakus-universe/mankind-has-stopped-evolving

[51] Ruiz Rejón, M, 2017, The Origin of the Human Species: a Chromosome Fusion? https://www.bbvaopenmind.com/en/the-origin-of-the-human-species-a-chromosome-fusion/

[52] Stankiewicz, P., 2016, One pedigree we all may have come from – did Adam and Eve have the chromosome 2 fusion? https://www.ncbi.nlm.nih.gov/pmc/articles/PMC5037601/

[53] Briggs, H., 2016, DNA clue to how humans evolved big brains http://www.bbc.com/news/science-environment-38226810

[54] Smithsonian, Bigger Brains: Complex Brains for a Complex World http://humanorigins.si.edu/human-characteristics/brains

[55] Ghose, T., 2015, "Big Brain" Gene Allowed for Evolutionary Expansion of Human Neocortex https://www.scientificamerican.com/article/big-brain-gene-allowed-for-evolutionary-expansion-of-human-neocortex/

[56] PA, 2012, What made us human: 'unique' evolution gene found https://www.smh.com.au/technology/what-made-us-human-unique-evolution-gene-found-20121115-29d9p.html

[57] Trafton, A., 2014, Neuroscientists identify key role of language gene http://news.mit.edu/2014/language-gene-0915

[58] Earliest known fossil of the genus Homo dates to 2.8 to 2.75 million years ago https://www.heritagedaily.com/2015/03/earliest-known-fossil-genus-homo-dates-2-8-2-75-million-years-ago/106958

[59] Dennis, M. Y., 2012, Human-specific evolution of novel SRGAP2 genes by incomplete segmental duplication

https://www.ncbi.nlm.nih.gov/pmc/articles/PMC3365555/

[60] Griffith, J., 2015, Freedom: The End of the Human Condition, Sexual selection for integrativeness explains neoteny
https://www.humancondition.com/freedom-sexual-selection-for-integration-explains-neoteny/

[61] Trut, L., 2009, Animal evolution during domestication: the domesticated fox as a model
https://www.ncbi.nlm.nih.gov/pmc/articles/PMC2763232/

[62] Universidad de Barcelona, 2018, Did humans domesticate themselves?
http://www.ub.edu/web/ub/en/menu_eines/noticies/2018/02/027.html

[63] Rojas, A., 2010, UFO disclosure at Kirtland Air Force Base
http://www.openminds.tv/ufo-discosure-afb/3818

35417317R00100

Printed in Great Britain
by Amazon